Financial Troubleshooting

An Action Plan for Money Management in Small and Growing Businesses

by David H. Bangs Jr.

and Michael Pellecchia

Inc. Business Resources
Boston, Massachusetts

Published by *Inc.* Business Resources,
a division of Goldhirsh Group, Inc.,
publisher of *Inc.* magazine.
Copyright © 1999 by Goldhirsh Group, Inc.,
Boston, Mass. All rights reserved.

Editorial Director: Bradford W. Ketchum, Jr.
Copy Editor: Audra Mulhearn
Design: IBR Creative Services Group

This book is based on *Financial Troubleshooting: An Action Plan for Money Management in
the Small Business*, which was originally edited by David H. Bangs, Jr., and published by Upstart
Publishing Co., Inc., a division of Dearborn Publishing Group, Inc. All rights to the title and
material were acquired by Goldhirsh Group, Inc., in 1998, when the book was updated and
revised by Michael Pellecchia and Bradford W. Ketchum, Jr.

This publication is designed to provide accurate and authoritative information with regard to
the subject matter covered. It is sold with the understanding that the publisher is not engaged in
rendering legal, accounting, or other professional service. If legal advice or other expert assistance
is required, the services of a competent professional should be sought.

ISBN 1-880394-92-8

Printed in the United States of America

Contents

FOREWORD

I n their original form as a collection of articles in *Common Sense Management Techniques*, the topics in this book were recognized widely as key tools for small-business financial managers. Later, they were assembled in book form to comprise the first edition of *Financial Troubleshooting*. Since then, these topics have maintained their important standing in the viability of start-ups and growing small businesses, particularly for owner/managers who do not have a financial background.

This new edition treats the topics under the book title of *Financial Troubleshooting* as an integrated whole. While updating many of the topics, the book maintains its original approach, advocating caution in all aspects of small-business financial management.

The landscape of banking and small business has changed during the 1990s, but some things remain true as ever. As author David H. Bangs Jr. pointed out in the original edition, in 1992:

1. Simple things work best.
2. Positive cash flow equals survival.
3. Forecasting and planning help make profitable businesses. These activities also please bankers and help build strong foundations for growth.
4. Businesses that use tight, carefully thought-out budgets will succeed. If they stumble, they can be picked up, dusted off, and sent forward—but

businesses without budgets will collapse without a chance to redeem themselves.

5. Small-business owners who want to work with bankers have to spend a certain amount of time with numbers.

This book covers most aspects of financial controls that a small-business owner will use. They are derived from common sense, and any additional structure and detail are not designed to make work for bookkeepers and accountants, but more so to help the owner develop a management strategy that accounts for all the finances in a business and how they relate to operations as well.

Even with an outside or inside professional setting up the chart of accounts and other accounting books, business owners will want to be comfortable with the tools for record keeping, sorting, summarizing, and analyzing the information from business transactions.

The tools presented here are part of the basic business vocabulary, yet many of us avoid the use of analytical tools. The small-business person today does so at his or her own risk. Technology is causing changes in many cost structures. For example, who would have guessed 15 years ago that telephone costs would undergo a profound change, not only in the pricing structures, but in the types and importance of services offered? The same is true for computers and other technology-based tools.

One great byproduct of crunching numbers as they come in is to spot problems early on. A great deal of comfort can be derived from sensing future trends accurately before they balloon out of control. It's worth the trouble to set up systems in advance. And it's absolutely essential to do so if your financing comes from outside sources.

Users of this book may follow in the footsteps of previous readers who, upon reading *Financial Troubleshooting*, got a reality check on the records of their business transactions. If you are starting out in small business, this book will help you gain perspective on what is to come. There is no substitute—not even within these pages—for good help from professional accountants and bankers. In this day and age, recruiting the best help you can find is essential to building the foundation for financial success.

Michael Pellecchia
Revision Author
Fort Worth, Texas

CHAPTER 1

Organizing Your Information Needs

W e live in an era of rapid change. Once it may have been possible to run a solid business on hunch and habit, because the rate of change was slow enough to enable a company, once set on the right path, to continue down that path with little danger. Not any more.

Every business generates a stream of information. The prosperous business, the carefully managed growing business, uses that information as an integral part of the managerial strategy.

Decisions often rely on hunch, habit, information, and any combination of the three. Hunches are fine: They provide insights into your business, encourage you to enter new markets in spite of apparent obstacles, and perform an energizing function. However, for every hunch that does succeed, many do not. The hunch tempered by information gains you the best of both worlds. Your hunch is a reflection of your experience and intelligence, and the information is a backup.

Habits are also fine. They save time and free us up to do more than we could do otherwise. But if we don't question our habits from time to time, then we are not using information in its best way.

Rather than risk disaster (assuming that these are major decisions), you need to have a reasonable information base on which to test your hunches and habits before charging ahead. Over time, your decisions will only be as good as the information you base them on.

Ensuring a clear, consistent, and coherent information flow is not an easy task. All of us get so close to our own businesses that we have trouble seeing the forest for the trees. That's where outside experts can be invaluable. Accountants, consultants, and software can help set up information systems that work for your kind of business.

Your information needs will vary in cost, timeliness, level of detail, and applicability. To make the best use of your time, you need organized, concise information that sums up the activities of your company in a useful way.

The five steps of organizing your information needs will help you get what you need, when you need it—at a price and level of detail that makes sense for your company.

Outline the 10 Most Important Decisions

The first step in establishing the right information flow for your business is to take a close look at the important decisions that your business faces in the near future. As a practical exercise, this has several benefits.

First, it's an excellent planning tool. All of us have a number of decisions we are expected to make, some of which are more important than others. Yet if you're anything like the rest of us, you seldom take time to rank the decisions in terms of potential impact, importance, and long-term effects.

Second, as you list the 10 most important decisions you face, you will probably find that the first 5 or 6 are obvious. The remainder take a bit more thought.

Check over your completed list, and ask yourself the following questions:
- Can I make a decision on the information I have available? Would more information help?
- Ideally, what kind of information would I use to make these decisions?
- Practically speaking, can I get that information? How? When? At what cost?
- What is the minimum amount of information I need to make the right decision?

Next, rank the decisions in terms of long-range impact, since this will help focus your attention on the more important problems. Ask yourself: What major decision have I been putting off? Why?

Most of us know that there are decisions that for one reason or another we are avoiding. These can include financial decisions (Can we afford to expand?), strategic decisions (Should we open a branch office?), and emotionally painful decisions (Should I fire Harvey?). In all major decisions, well-organized information will make a positive difference.

Your list need not be exhaustive or perfect. The purpose of the list (and of the questions the list will raise) is to help you fit the proper information flow for your company based on your knowledge of its operations and goals. For entrepreneurs, goals may revolve around issues of personal aspirations, building a business that can run in the owner's absence, and how much risk can be tolerated along the way.

You'll train yourself to distinguish between critical and ordinary issues. With the list of potential decisions in hand, look at the next step of organizing information.

List Activities to Monitor

What activities go on in your business? The challenge is to see how these activities fit together—and what they involve that doesn't show up at first glance. Examples of the kinds of activities you need to control are cash flow, sales/marketing activities, and production.

Cash flow is straightforward: If you spend more than you take in, sooner or later the negative cash flow will kill the business. But, if you consistently take in more than you spend, the positive cash flow will let you pay dividends. Building an entrepreneurial organization requires reinvesting profits in infrastructure and sales and marketing, while postponing payoffs. Production activities absorb a large portion of expenses, requiring close monitoring.

Collect Accurate Data

Raw data is generated by any attempt to record what happens in a business. Usually, activities are measured in terms of money, units, or time. Cash flow is measured in dollars and time; the idea is to learn how cash in motion operates. To keep tabs on new sales personnel, you need call reports and sales information. The orders are a further source of raw data, letting you know what is selling and who is buying.

Many off-the-shelf software programs speed the process of collecting and organizing data, and the human touch of an accountant can still have far-

Start with a Decision Checklist

Here are key decisions for a restaurant start-up, for example, prioritized according to potential impact, importance, and long-term effects.

- ☐ Trademark name and concept
- ☐ Determine build-out costs, food costs, facility and operating expenses
- ☐ Secure bank financing (lowest possible rate)
- ☐ Develop recipes and menu
- ☐ Hire a contractor(s)
- ☐ Complete construction
- ☐ Marketing in advance of grand opening
- ☐ Hiring and staffing
- ☐ Shakedown/trial-run period
- ☐ Formal opening

reaching implications for your final information flow. Example: If your chart of accounts is not done well, it can be worse than useless. You don't want to get stuck with a chart of accounts that doesn't reflect your business and your goals. Most prepackaged charts of accounts can be modified and customized, and a first-rate accountant will make certain that your chart of accounts fits your business. (*See Chapter 2, "Recruiting an Accountant," for ideas on how to locate the right one for your business.*)

Case: Granite Rock Relies on Three Sources

Granite Rock Co. is a $100-million company that produces and sells crushed stone, asphalt, and other heavy construction materials. Located in Watsonville, Calif., it gathers, analyzes, and acts on information from at least three sources:

- *Customers.* In its annual surveys, Granite Rock asks customers to rate the company against its competition. The company also holds periodic focus groups to probe for ideas about new products and services.

- *Company operations.* The chief financial officer tracks changes in the aging of receivables, in the time it takes to turn around a credit application, in the accuracy of the company's sales invoices, and in on-time delivery of operating statements. The transportation manager gathers survey data about on-time delivery, drivers' attitudes, and the time it takes customers to load up and get back on the road.

- *The outside world.* Employees are welcome to attend "Graniterock University" on company time. These meetings include outside speakers and suppliers with technical presentations. Company teams also make numerous benchmarking trips to other companies, including those outside the industry. "We exchanged statistics with Domino's Pizza," notes Bruce Woolpert, copresident and CEO. "We learned from them some places to get better maps. Then we hired some college students to pencil in street numbers on the maps. Domino's does that."

Most important, Granite Rock acts on the information it gathers. It assigns teams to share and analyze information, then to find and follow solutions. All the experience and information find their way into training current and future employees.

Organize the Data

Raw data need considerable shaping before you can use them. As the information is generated, it needs to be summarized. For most businesses, this requires standard financial statements: balance sheets, profit-and-loss statements, cash flow analyses and budgets, and perhaps deviation analyses for the financial controls.

Most of us are familiar with these statements, though sometimes we forget that they are meant to be used to show how our business is performing. We're often guilty of the error of putting the financials aside "until we have time for them." Learning about a problem or an opportunity too late is no way to run a business. One of the criteria for measuring the adequacy of our performance is to see how quickly we can identify and capitalize on new opportunities—and how quickly we can solve problems.

For sales/marketing control, you need a way of summarizing the salesperson's performance on either a monthly or weekly basis, as seems indicated. Ask for a summary of calls made and orders placed, and a report on customer suggestions, criticisms, and other ideas.

For any personnel decisions, some basic information is mandatory. To evaluate people fairly, document what they do. What about attendance? Ever try to fire someone for poor attendance and then not be able to provide the dates involved? The data needed may be exceptions: "Absent for 18 consecutive Fridays..." The summary form should cover the aspects of performance that are most important, otherwise it won't be useful or used.

Use the Data

The final step is interpreting the data and putting it to work. Cash flow reports, for example, are not informative by themselves. They must be compared to some standard—that is, interpreted—before they become informative.

That's your job. The initial data gathering and compilation can (and in most cases should) be delegated. Using the data is a different matter. This task cannot be safely or lightly given to someone else.

The financial and other summaries contain a huge amount of information to help you manage your business. Your accountant or your bookkeeper can't apply the information, and they can't use it to manage your business.

Your time is limited. As the owner/manager, you can only look at the summaries—the tip of the iceberg. If they show some deviation (worse or better than usual), you might then have to get into the details. Otherwise, trust the details to the systems of information collection you've set up. That's why careful systems are set up in the first place. You have enough to do as it is.

Look for deviations first, trends second. If the cash flow gets sticky, monitor the details—daily, in some cases, rather than monthly or quarterly. If sales are slow, pay the same attention to daily sales reports. If production is stalled for some reason, give it immediate attention—no product means no sales, no cash flow.

But remember: All the data in the world won't do you any good if you don't have standards by which to measure projected cash flow, actual balance between receivables and payables, current and historical sales and marketing data, and product and production information. That's why the forms of analysis described in chapters 9 through 11 are so important. Most managers can find the root cause of failures before they happen and take advantage of unexpected windfalls by plotting current against historical actual sales, revenues, and operating statistics. Computer software enables this to be done with more detail and less bias.

Implement Information Flow—and Review Regularly

As a managerial strategy, using information flow as outlined in the preceding steps is a version of management by exception. You set the standards, based on your knowledge and experience. Your business plan probably states many of them clearly: sales per month, cash flow and budgeting figures, personnel policies on vacations, days off, and sick pay, to name a few. When an exception occurs, you want to know why.

Make your information-flow system a managerial priority item to be reviewed carefully at least annually, and review and adjust your strategy whenever there is a major change in your business.

How much time does it take to implement a careful information-flow strategy? There are tons of literature on the subject, and all kinds of consultants are available to help for a fee. Some typical cost-effective resources are:

- Trade journals and association publications
- Books and magazines (e.g., *Inc.*) on small business
- Your accountant and banker
- Local libraries
- Area colleges and universities
- Small Business Development Centers (partially funded by the SBA and administered at the state or local level, usually through universities, chambers of commerce, and other business organizations)
- Small Business Resource Center at www.webcom.com (provides a library of downloadable files on business planning and raising capital, with a focus on home-based businesses)

- Business and trade associations, such as the Council of Smaller Enterprise (COSE), in Cleveland; Smaller Business Association of New England, in Waltham, Mass.; and National Association of Women Business Owners (NAWBO), based in Silver Spring, Md. (For trade- or industry-specific organizations, consult Gale Research's *Encyclopedia of Associations*.)
- The Small Business Administration's SCORE and SBI programs (see "Resources" on page 165)
- Internet resources on small business (see page 169)

How do you formulate an information strategy? Return to the first step: What are the 10 most important decisions you have to make during the next year? By now, you can ask what summary information would help make those decisions better and work backward. For example, to make good cash flow decisions, you need to have financial statements, including balance sheets, profit-and-loss statements, cash flow reports, and budgets. These statements will depend on accurate sales and cost figures, which in turn will be generating analytical questions such as, "Are we getting the right/reasonable amount of return from our most profitable customers? What are they telling us? Are there other products we can develop for them? For allied markets?"

In addition to working backward from the decision list to determine what summary information you will need, your actual information flow can help you look ahead to future decisions. The interdependence of information and activity helps you manage the activities of your business better.

Once again: What decisions are you facing? What information would help make those decisions easier or better? Can you get that information? If not, what can you do to get that information (within the bounds of cost and time)?

Use your information flow. It makes your hunches better, helps you see which habits are good and which are harmful, and it will prove itself on your bottom line.

Summary

Information is only useful if you use it—and if it is accurate. When assessing your information needs, keep timeliness and cost in view. Too much detail will get you bogged down; too little and you will run unnecessary risks.

Your aim is to manage by exception: The reports (organized data) should be compared to standards and action taken only when there is a reason to take action. Look into deviations only when they are sizable enough to warrant your attention.

For examples of information flow and an action plan, see page 12.

Identify Activities _____

Purchasing	Stocking	Collecting	Paying
Producing	Marketing	Borrowing	Planning
Scheduling	Controlling	Hiring	Selling

Measure Raw Data _____

Sales	Cost of selling	Overhead
Cost of materials	Units of product produced	Timing
Employee attendance	Employee performance	

Organize Data _____

Balance sheet	Production reports	Attendance
Income statement	Ratios	Acid test
Trends	Sales reports	

Compare with Standards _____

Historical	Industrial	Projections
Experience	Insight	Government

Analyze Results of Comparison (new information) _____

Liquidity is low, leverage high	Inside sales staff frequently late or absent
Receivables high/old, payables okay	Employee turnover high
Sales low, profits low	

Make Decisions and Implement Action _____

Improve collection procedure
Identify strong and weak sales personnel
Control extravagant selling costs, improve marketing
Purchase and stock in economic units

Action Plan

Organizing Information Needs

❏ Outline and prioritize the 10 most important decisions you have to make.
❏ List the business activities you want to monitor. Collect accurate data.
❏ Organize the data in standard forms (such as financial statements, call reports, and order lists).
❏ Use the data. Schedule time to review the information regularly.
❏ Implement information flow; review it periodically.

CHAPTER 2

Recruiting an Accountant

Your choice of an accountant is extremely important. As with any consultants, the value of accountants depends on how you use them. And more than ever before, accounting professionals are called upon to help with tasks that formerly were considered to be on the fringes of finance, like marketing and production. Accountants are also major players in the world of junk bond financing, leveraged buyouts, takeover defenses, company reorganizations, consolidation, international operations, and government reporting.

What You Should Know about CPAs

Selection of the right accounting help for small business is crucial. The first tip to remember: Don't put off looking for an accountant until you need one. Everyone needs an accountant during tax time and other busy seasons, like fiscal period closings. If you want to set up interviews with several accountants prior to narrowing down your selections, allow plenty of time flexibility.

There are some things you can do—and know—to make your mission much easier. Knowledge of the profession, skillful preparation, proper selection procedures, and good communication—plus some chemistry—will help ease the search.

Accounting is a formal means of gathering data for the purpose of external and internal financial reporting, planning, and control of business operations. Another way to put it: Accounting produces information about the economic behavior generated by a firm's activities within its environment.

In the United States, accounting evolved from management control to politicization. Annual reports up until 1933 reflected management's view completely. From 1933 until 1973, accounting principles were encouraged by the Securities and Exchange Commission (SEC) and developed by professional bodies. Since 1973, the Financial Accounting Standards Board (FASB) and others have brought accounting into the public sector, with the idea that accounting numbers affect economic behavior, and thus practices and standards should be accountable to the public. Now, every state certifies public accountants. The U.S. Department of Labor estimates that there are some 900,000 accountants, about a third of them certified.

Check Those Credentials

Certification is rigorous, and would-be CPAs must first earn a bachelor's degree. The new graduate must then sit for the Uniform CPA Examination. The grueling two-and-a-half-hour exam, prepared and graded by the American Institute of Certified Public Accountants (AICPA), covers theory and practice of auditing and accounting, as well as aspects of business law and taxes. The test is given twice a year in the 50 states, the District of Columbia, Puerto Rico, the Virgin Islands, and Guam.

Individual state boards of accountancy grant the CPA certification. They also issue licenses to practice required of CPAs who practice publicly on their own or in accounting firms. The license is not required of CPAs who work in education, government, or private industry. In a majority of states, CPAs who practice publicly must also complete 40 hours of continuing professional education—known in CPA shorthand as CPEs—every year. The CPEs may come through conferences, seminars, or special courses. Some states also require CPAs to meet an experience requirement. For example, in Michigan, a CPA must earn a B.A. with a concentration in accounting, pass the CPA exam, and have two years of public accounting experience.

Degree, exam, and experience accounted for, the new CPA typically seeks work. Accounting firms generally recruit on campus, seeking the cream of the campus crop. Some create internships, then hire from that pool. Many hire new M.B.A.s.

Many accounting firms now hire individuals from nonaccounting programs. For example, one firm has 40 full-time investigators, many with law enforcement experience, in its national fraud and forensic practice.

Every week, payroll administrator Betty Chunco spent Monday and Tuesday totaling work hours from Micro Stamping's 145 hourly time cards and typing that information into a computer. And every week, she'd have to double-check and recalculate the numbers when the totals on the time cards came out wrong because of calculation and data-entry errors. Micro Stamping, based in Somerset, N.J., has a union payroll involving "a lot of calculations based on hours people work," according to human-resources manager Frank Semcer Jr. That includes overtime and vacation pay based on hours worked.

The company had been using software called Caelus to track work hours billable to particular projects. For general hours (and total work hours), though, employees still had to use time cards. This led to expensive and error-prone handwork in transcribing and tracking work hours.

Now, with new software called the TC-1 Labor Management System, from Datamatics Management Services, Micro Stamping has eliminated the manual steps. Instead of punching a time card, employees swipe a bar-coded identity tag through an ATM-like machine to gain access to the building, and with another swipe, begin or end their official workday.

Says Semcer, "I can now print a report that gives me total hours worked by all employees, or copy it to disk and put it into Excel." Payroll processing time has been cut in half, with an estimated savings in accounting labor of $300 each week.

Historically, large CPA firms concentrated their services with larger businesses, and small accounting firms focused their services on small businesses. By custom and tradition, businesses rarely changed accountants. But changing times have called for large and small firms alike to reconsider traditions in light of recent workplace trends.

Although a sudden spike in growth can turn a small company into a medium-sized company in short order, most stable small businesses will not have a lot of work for an accountant to do. Such a business can manage most of its basic financial records without the necessity of an accountant, by either setting up a simple, inexpensive manual system of bookkeeping or by using software, such as M.Y.O.B. and Quicken (or QuickBooks or Peachtree Accounting for more complex businesses, such as those with inventory).

If you do go this route, have a pro review your system to make sure your records clearly reflect your income and expenses. Using ledger sheets, you can set up a chart of accounts listing cash, credit card, and check expenses, with columns listing the types of expenditures. All expenses should be listed by category rather than time period. It's up to the business owner whether to run totals daily, weekly, or monthly. And every item listed should have a paper backup such as an invoice, cash voucher, receipt, or check register.

Software records usually echo the way handwritten books would be set up, only they look a lot nicer. And they also automate double-entry book-keeping, which can be pretty time-consuming if done manually. Either a DOS, Windows, or Macintosh computer can be used to post accounts, retrieve information by date, category, or other characteristic, and print out reports.

It's no wonder then that accountants and bookkeepers wouldn't want to compete with software that does what they do, only cheaper. As a result, more number-crunchers are offering many different types of professional services, including customized software design and installation, teams set up especially to solve small-business problems, financial planning seminars for spouses, or training sessions on tax and financial topics.

At the same time, there are non-CPA professionals who may offer busi-ness-specific solutions or tax specialization. Though not certified, many have received rigorous training, such as the "enrolled agents" who combine tax preparation expertise with knowledge of how the IRS works.

Bookkeeper vs. Accountant

We asked Stephen E. Johns to provide an overview on accounting systems for a business wishing to do government contracting. Based in Fort Worth, Johns has practiced as an enrolled agent for 18 years.

"A small subcontractor is going to need a formal accounting system for satisfying his bonding requirements in many cases. His books may actually be subject to review by government agencies," says Johns. "If you don't hire a bookkeeper in-house, then you need to hire an outside bookkeeper. And you need to draw some distinctions between bookkeepers and accountants. The first step is having the formal set of books. The second step is making sure those books are maintained properly. And that's the job of the accountant. So you end up with two people on your advisory staff: the bookkeeper who's doing the work and the accountant who comes in and reviews the material to determine if it meets the requirements.

"A small manufacturer normally will not have a cost accountant on staff. The internal auditor will normally review what the bookkeeping department is doing. You then hire a CPA firm to perform the independent audit function. It comes in and reviews what the bookkeeping department and internal auditor and management are doing with the company. Depending on the engagement parameters, this may be a review or an audit.

"Inventory accounting is always industry specific. Once you get beyond the very small business, you need to be into the more industry-specific software. QuickBooks is an excellent accounting package for a small business in its beginning stages. Once your business grows to be a 'large' small business, you've probably outgrown what QuickBooks can do for you, and you then need to go to something that's more expensive and can handle a more specific manufacturing process tracking."

Knowing When to Get Help

"Stable businesses providing unchanging products to customers with unswerving loyalties may not need accounting services beyond basic bookkeeping," notes Irving L. Blackman, a frequently published CPA and senior partner in Blackman Kallick Bartelstein, a large Chicago accounting firm. And most small-business owners can handle daily record maintenance of income, expenses, and capital expenditures.

Still, accountants can be indispensable when it comes time to close the books, prepare financial statements or tax returns, and help with budgeting. Even though software can generate excellent reports, accountants can offer extra advantages. In private businesses, for example, three to four years of audited financial statements are a must when owners get ready to sell.

Many companies are adapting to the new competitive environment by using their accountants to do more than deal with accounting, audit, and tax issues. Management accounting is now just as likely to focus on process improvement and product and customer profitability, as it once did on cost control and vertical reporting. Some of the newer ideas, such as cost-led pricing, revenue management, and activity-based costing, contain powerful tools for streamlining company operations.

Like bookkeeping, many management accounting functions are now available via computer systems and databases. Managers who know their way around accounting reports may find little need for an in-person accountant, so the profession is learning to ask the right questions and do things that automation cannot do.

Some signs of needing an accountant are obvious, for example, when your company confronts growth, economic or technological change, unfamiliar markets, new laws, tax complications, the need for a bank loan or outside financing, or a more demanding or dynamic environment.

And when it comes to tax and regulations, governments look at all size businesses with the same jaundiced eyes. That reason alone makes the accountant's bill seem quite cost-effective if and when the IRS comes to call.

Making the Perfect Match

Under such conditions, marrying the right accountant to your business is crucial, and the selection decision becomes key. Take these steps as you look for a partner for your financial future:

1. *Know your needs first, based on where your business will be next month, next year, even five years from now.* Compile a list of problems you'd like solved, improvements you'd like made, equipment you need to purchase, profits you'd like to generate.

A skilled accountant can ask questions that will draw out problems—and perhaps potential solutions—from you. "A skillful accountant will really find out what you've got in your head," says CPA Blackman.

Try to establish where problems exist and how a CPA can help. "The more you know beforehand, the better off you'll be," says Sam Hoyt, director of media relations for the 240,000-member American Institute of Certified Public Accountants (AICPA).

2. *Consult with friends, colleagues, or business associates for CPAs they can recommend.* "The best way to find a CPA is through references from friends or business associates who use one and are pleased with one," suggests Varley Simons, vice-president of the Chicago-based American Society of Women CPAs and a partner in the Atlanta accounting firm of Gorbandt and Simons.

Seek out leads from other business owners in your industry or from associations representing your trade or profession. Check with your banker, lawyer, or state CPA society.

Some business publications and Internet Web sites issue their own directories of accountants and other financial professionals, grouped by state, locality, or specialization. The search engine Excite, for example, will generate a list of accountants in your zip code.

3. *Compare the advantages—and disadvantages—of a large firm with a national reputation and a small firm with a local following.* Contrast their services with your needs. "Don't necessarily be influenced by someone who tells you big is best," says Hoyt. The accounting firm you select should be one that is specifically targeting businesses your size. Interview the person who will be working with you to make sure you will be able to develop a rapport. Look for a firm that is familiar with—or can quickly learn—the kind of work you need done.

Kiva Container, in Phoenix, makes boxes from corrugated paper and cardboard primarily for manufacturers of consumer goods. When the company sought financing for a new plant in South Carolina, its bank cited a pair of recent operating losses and asked for more accountancy, including monthly financial reports rather than the customary quarterly or semiannual ones. The bank also sought to step up the CPA's reporting from a not-very-stringent "compilation" to a more expensive and tougher "review" engagement. On top of that, the bank asked for financial projections four years into the future. Even though Kiva had been doing business with the same bank for eight years, arranging financing for the South Carolina plant took five months, including the reams of documentation that had to be generated.

---

4. *Set up a personal interview.* Ask in advance if fees are charged for the first consultation. Some CPAs levy charges; others may not or may waive fees if you retain them. Find out the basis for their ongoing fees.

Use the interview to ask questions and gather information you most need to know. Ask about education, professional experience, and personal qualifications that pertain to your needs. Study qualifications before the interview, if possible, then structure the interview around questions about them.

Some considerations: study at an accredited institution, experience in methods and procedures, management consulting, contact with executives, or experience developing, implementing, and installing specialized programs.

You may also want to evaluate evidence of personal initiative, verbal and written communication skills, ability to obtain and analyze facts, diligence, and use of imagination in solving small-business problems.

Before the interview, devise a method for capturing information key to your final decision. A simple rating system may be helpful. You may want to include space for summary comments and any conclusions you've reached.

Allow sufficient time to complete your questioning, and convey interest and consideration for experienced professionals. Be courteous: Don't burn bridges in communicating your final decision.

5. *Ask for references.* "They should be checked too," advises Blackman. References don't always help you make the right match. "But it might help you not pick the wrong one," he says.

Here's what you need to consider when choosing accounting software:
1. **Auditing features.** These might include a map mode, annotation of formulas as text notes, and annotations using text boxes attached to the corresponding drawing layers. The user should be able to display antecedents and consequences of formulas.
2. **Data import/export.** Spreadsheets should be able to import or export files with a number of different database formats.
3. **Database screens.** You should be able to develop customized data entry screens, to search and replace data, and to sort, query, and analyze extensively.
4. **Recalculation.** If your spreadsheet can do several different types of recalculation and also do recalculation in the background, you will save a lot of time.
5. **Formatting.** Your spreadsheet should allow the creation of defined numeric formats and custom currency symbols.

Other important spreadsheet features to look for are two- and three-dimensional chart support, text file support, macro recorders, model building, printing, and timed backup and other security features.

If your business has more than $500,000 in annual revenues, consider the following features:
1. **Customization.** Users should have customized menus, data entry, and lookup facilities. Vendors should provide source code.
2. **Support.** General ledger should support intercompany postings, perform allocations, and perform and report on multicurrency conversions and transactions.
3. **Payables.** Accounts payable should be able to flag 1099 items, post intercompany vouchers, and allocate eight characters to a vendor number. It should also be able to calculate commissions.
4. **Ordering.** The order entry module should be able to place orders by using your customers' part numbers, allow drop shipments, and track customers' request dates as line items.
5. **Inventory control.** Inventory should report slow-moving or obsolete items, price items by classes, and track items by serial number or lot number. Inventory modules should support all necessary costing methods and report on unit costs and reorders.

6. *When you make your final selection, ask for an engagement letter.* Most CPAs now charge by the hour, and any accountant should provide you with the letter, spelling out duties and fees. Make sure you have the right to approve any extra work before the extra fee is calculated and billed.

Services provided by a senior-level partner may be more costly than those provided by a staff member. Those requiring frequent, detailed, or customized reports may be more costly than routine statements at widely spaced intervals. CPAs in major cities may be more expensive than those in rural areas.

Key Questions to Ask a Prospective CPA

The worst way to find a CPA is to "call one up and hire him," sight unseen, Blackman believes. He recommends that every candidate be asked the same questions. Among his key questions to ask:

• *Is timely service delivered?* Accounting information can get out of date quickly. Except for annual information, most accounting information should be no more than 10 to 30 days old.

• *Will the same people always service your account?* Who else in the firm will be available for second opinions?

• *What services beyond the usual reporting and number-crunching are offered?*

• *How can the accountant help you make money?* It sounds like a wise-guy question, but the answer will help you find out if candidates are interested in your business. Did they review the financial information you provided prior to the interview? Did they make sure you understood the accounting concepts, instead of just tossing off a bunch of jargon?

• *How are fees structured and calculated?* The accounting firm should be able to quote a specified amount geared toward the format and time frame in which you submit your raw data.

CPAs are urged to maintain good client relations, extend prompt service, take a sincere interest in clients, avoid arguments, return phone calls promptly, and treat clients as equals. You may certainly ask about the time frame for returning calls.

Chemistry Should Click

Despite your best efforts to evaluate a CPA's technical skills and ability, chemistry can count in the end. A CPA will ultimately become intimately familiar with your firm's finances—in good times and in bad ones. "You're going to want somebody you can work with," notes the AICPA's Hoyt.

"As the world turns, more small businesses are likely to turn to accountants for management that fits broadly into a financial framework," says futurist Hank E. Koehn, president of the Los Angeles-based Trimtab Consulting Group. "The action is in consulting services. Because of the trust that binds a business owner/operator to an accountant, the financial professional is in a unique position to offer advice on a variety of management issues."

Koehn forecasts that accountants will try to establish more personal relationships with clients, make new attempts to offer creative solutions to small-business problems, and more aggressively extend services to small businesses. Accountants may have a greater role in small-business decision making, helping to identify, package, and price services or recommend and install computer systems or software. Their financial planning services will increase. More may become specialists where specific industry needs can be targeted.

Because there are realistically a limited number of "billable" hours, fees may become more flexible, with some "unbundled" or specially packaged fees, Koehn predicts.

Whatever the future for the accounting profession, there are times when an otherwise stable CPA/business relationship can sour. Signals of trouble: inability to reach your accountant by phone, phone calls not returned, questions not completely answered, frequent mistakes.

If your dissatisfaction persists and your CPA does not take steps to remedy its causes, file a written complaint with the appropriate state board of accountancy and with the AICPA. The AICPA will examine the complaint and refer it to a regional trial board. If the complaint is warranted, sanctions can be levied against the accountant.

State boards of accountancy handle formal complaints similarly by reviewing them, seeking a CPA's response, and providing for appeals at each step up the sometimes lengthy ladder of administrative hearings and procedures. For the business seriously dissatisfied with its financial professional, another kind of professional may be called for—a lawyer who can take the complaint to court.

Summary

Besides informal (i.e., unpaid) advisers, you will need the advice of paid experts. These include an accountant, attorney, banker (paid indirectly), and insurance adviser. Your accountant should serve at least three functions:

1. Help you set up record-keeping systems, develop financial statements, and prepare tax returns.
2. Keep you informed of how the tax laws affect your business.
3. Assist you in complying with your tax-related obligations as an employer (e.g., Social Security, unemployment, and pension plans).

As accountants position themselves to be of greater service to their small-business clients, they are offering a wider variety of services. Here's a list of some you may want to ask about:

Management Reporting and Analysis

- Maintenance of all tax records
- Tax preparation
- Management reporting, including data for policy and operating decisions, profit-and-loss statements, trend calculations, and inventory information
- Financial controls, including credit policies and work necessary for securing outside funds
- Corporate location, examining location needs, capital budget requirements, handling mergers and acquisitions, advising on return-on-investment considerations
- Inventory management, such as order quantity, cost calculation and computerization
- Ability to provide information on a timely and consistent basis about changes in tax laws and financial reporting requirements
- Monitoring and evaluation of revenues and expenses as compared to business concerns of similar size and nature
- Training seminars or workshops on financial planning, retirement planning, and other financial management issues. Seminars cosponsored with banks or brokerage houses
- Computerized audits
- Evaluation of investment opportunities

Budgeting and Cash Flow

- Budgeting and profit planning, including long-range forecasting and break-even analysis
- Cost accounting and reporting
- Cost control, reduction, and prevention
- Clerical cost reduction
- Advice on cash requirements for certain stated periods, budget forecasting, borrowing management, business organization, taxes, and potential trouble spots

(continued on page 24)

Record Keeping and Control

- Personnel administration in such areas as job evaluation, recruiting, employee incentives, compensation, pension plans, and employee benefits
- Design and implementation of data processing systems for payroll, invoice, and credit information
- Analysis of filing and records management with recommendations about centralized or decentralized records and record-retention methods
- Improvements in paperwork flow and procedures manuals
- Data maintenance, interpretation, and recommendations resulting from interpretations
- Financial and record-keeping software that can give you accounts receivable, order entry/invoicing, and inventory management information
- Invoice design
- Computer system design

Market Trends and Analysis

- Forecasting of market trends, sales, and consumer attitudes
- Marketing expense control
- Production planning and scheduling
- Surveys of client satisfaction
- Awareness of trends affecting your business and theirs

Action Plan

Recruiting an Accountant

❑ Know your needs and goals first, before you seek an accountant.

❑ Consult with friends, colleagues, and business associates. Whom do they recommend? Do any names come up more than others?

❑ Compare the advantages and disadvantages of using a large national firm or a small local firm.

❑ Set up a personal interview with several accountants. Make a choice between firms.

❑ Get an engagement letter from the firm you select.

CHAPTER 3

Using Economic Forecasts

Business activities typically happen in an atmosphere of uncertainty. In order to plan ahead and budget into the future, the risk of uncertainty should be minimized. That's why forecasts are used in every area of business, from departmental planning to overall management strategy.

Economic forecasts are notoriously inexact. No two economists seem to agree about anything, but it usually seems most of them are partially right. Even when basic economic information is "spun" for political expediency, your competitors, suppliers, and customers will have a crowd reaction to it. So economic forecasting has an effect both inside and outside the business.

Macroeconomic variables, such as Gross Domestic Product (GDP), inflation, unemployment, interest rates, and exchange rates, influence our business environment. All businesses are affected, from the small office/home office market to corporate giants operating globally. Occasionally these economic forces affect different businesses in conflicting ways: An increased trade deficit, for example, means very different things to an importer and an exporter.

Business owners and managers should try to learn as much about economic variables as possible. The more you know—or can predict—about future economic conditions that affect your business, the greater your chances of preparing for and profiting from those conditions.

But how do you "get the goods": that knowledge of things to come?

That's easy—by forecasting. Some sources of data for making educated guesses are summarized on page 33. Using these educated guesses can help you predict future conditions.

Every business function is in some way affected by the level of and direction of change in economic variables. That is why you and the members of your management team should keep close track of key variables, such as GDP, unemployment rate, interest rate, foreign exchange rates, and inflation. These and other economic factors affect operations, marketing, and financial management.

Economic Forecasts and Operations

The operations manager deals primarily with the physical processes used to transform materials into the product. External forces do affect operations.

For example, changes in the level of the Gross Domestic Product (the value of all currently produced goods and services sold on the market during a particular time period) affect the operations manager in several ways. An increased GDP can result in higher personal disposable income. As personal disposable income rises, some economics experts say that the level of consumer purchases increases and creates a demand for more products and services. (This assumes, of course, that consumers' saving rates remain constant.) If the operations manager can base a materials requirement planning program on reliable forecasts for the firm's output, he or she will avoid scheduling headaches.

Work flow can then be planned in the smoothest, most efficient manner, consistent with the demand forecast. Further, if changes in the GDP signal sharp increases in demand for the firm's products, additional facilities or conversion to more efficient production techniques may be required. Alternatively, a drop in the GDP might suggest "tightening up the ship" to weather the coming economic storm.

Changes in the unemployment rate will determine not only the ease with which the operations manager will be able to adjust the company's workforce, but also will determine the quality of the workers he or she will be able to attract and hold at a given fixed pay rate. As the unemployment rate rises, the supply of available workers increases, affording the operations manager workers with a higher level of skills at the same price. At a lower unemployment rate, the operations manager may be forced to make do with less-skilled workers than he or she would normally choose.

Interest rates affect the operations manager in three ways. First, higher consumer interest rates may mean a drop in sales as credit purchases become more expensive. Production should be adjusted accordingly—expanding production if rates drop, or slowing production if interest rates increase.

Second, the operations manager could be impacted if rising interest rates make the cost of capital greater than the return on investment from operations. The operations manager could be squeezed for finances precisely at the same time that increased production to meet increasing sales places additional demands on the equipment.

And third, interest rates affect how much inventory is ordered and carried. Rising interest rates and lowered consumer demand could lead to a slow inventory turnover and unnecessary financial burdens for the business. Lower interest rates could reduce a business's carrying costs, encouraging the operations manager to increase inventory.

The foreign exchange rate primarily affects firms whose goods and services are sold overseas. As the dollar grows stronger relative to the currency of countries buying the firm's products, the operations manager faces two challenges. Foreign sales will decrease (causing higher inventories of finished goods) as the cost of domestic products climbs relative to the other country's currency. Domestic sales will also decrease as the price in dollars drops for competitive imports.

Conceivably, if the foreign competitor's increased sales are sufficient for it to increase production, competition for scarce resources may also drive up the competitor's cost and decrease its product's availability. In this case, the U.S. firm would enjoy an advantage—strong dollars in a competitive, international market for resources. The operations manager might stretch the advantage by relocating production overseas if the imbalance persists.

Economic Forecasts and Marketing

A business's marketing manager must find ways to get consumers to buy the company's product or service. Like the operations manager, the marketing manager should follow GDP because it reflects income and expenditure flows across all sectors of economic output located in the United States. Rising GDP growth should mean higher personal consumption expenditures and more sales for the firm.

However, the marketing manager must also determine the "mix" of goods or services available for sale. A certain amount of personal income must be reserved for spending on basic necessities, like food and shelter. Beyond that, marketing managers will need to forecast how much disposable income is available to buyers of consumer goods.

The unemployment rate will also influence how much income is available for spending, although this time the relationship is inverse. If the unemployment rate rises, personal income will fall. Again, expenditures (and thus demand) for luxury items will drop, and the marketing manager will need to promote more aggressively. A return to lower unemployment rates increases the market for purchases of discretionary items.

Interest rates affect the marketing manager in the area of credit purchases. As interest rates rise for the consumer, not only will the total price (purchase price plus interest) of the marketer's products rise, making them less attractive to consumers, but consumers could start saving more given the higher returns. This increase in saving reduces disposable income available for spending.

As noted earlier, the attractiveness of an international firm's goods in foreign markets will be affected by the exchange rate; domestic competition may heat up from imports made cheaper by a strong dollar. The marketing manager, with an accurate forecast of foreign exchange rates and a firm grasp of how they will affect the company's sales, can initiate damage control strategies before the damage becomes crippling. Further, the marketing manager should also watch for reverses that might suddenly make the company's products and services attractive in new markets.

Giving Owners the Big Picture

Here's how companies typically use economics in their shareholder communications:

From the 1997 Chemfirst Annual Report:

"We think 1998 continuing earnings will be up on a stronger second half. However, first-half results may be off due to some unusual events and lower custom manufacturing sales. We also have some price pressure from Asian semiconductor manufacturers and have seen a drop in Asian inquiries for Engineered Products and Services. We expect improvement in the Asian market with economic recovery there."

From the 1997 Annual Report of Cable Michigan:

"Several of Cable Michigan's service areas, such as the Ottawa-Kent County region and the Grand Traverse region in Michigan, are growing three times faster than the national average. The local economies we serve remain robust, with low unemployment and favorable demographics. Population increases and attendant new home construction continue to increase the aggregate size of our market."

Economic Forecasts and Financial Management

One job of the financial manager is ensuring that capital needed for production is available at the lowest cost. Cost can be measured directly as interest ("rent" for the use of the capital) and indirectly as opportunity costs (alternatives foregone as a result of choosing a particular course of action). To be an educated "buyer" of capital, the financial manager must closely follow the movements and relationships of economic variables.

Increases in the GDP generally signal increased demand. The financial manager should then be concerned with:

1. Making sure that the required capital is available at reasonable cost to finance increased production and,
2. Managing surplus cash to maximize wealth.

With forecasts of reduced GDP growth, the financial manager should develop strategies to counter the detrimental effects of reduced revenues.

Rising unemployment signals a probability of reduced sales and a possible additional problem for the financial manager. Government expenditures for unemployment compensation and other transfer payments affected by unemployment will increase; the government's appetite for capital will grow. This appetite can only be satisfied in three ways:

1. An increase in corporate taxes (which come out of a company's cash flow and directly reduce the undistributed profits available for reinvestment),
2. An increase in personal taxes (reducing personal disposable income available for buying the company's products), or
3. Deficit financing (when the government competes with the business sector for investment dollars and drives up interest rates).

Rising interest rates affect the financial manager not only by increasing the cost of capital, but also by altering the time horizon for investment decisions. Short-term and long-term funds require distinct investment, and borrowing costs can become onerous when interest rates change. So, the manager armed with interest rate forecasts can plan much better.

The financial manager's main concern with exchange rates is how much capital flows into and out of U.S. investments. A strong dollar attracts foreign investment to the United States, increasing funds available for investment and possibly reducing interest rates. A weak dollar has the opposite effect, and could cause interest rates to rise.

Every month, The Conference Board computes the composite indexes from the U.S. Department of Commerce. The leading indicators are followed closely by business executives and other decision makers. When the indicators change significantly, they signal that the economy is likely to change. In other words, the leading indicators are presumed to lead the economy and forecast where it is going. They are also important factors in determining the five macroeconomic variables explained in this chapter. The leading indicator approach to forecasting relies on detecting indicators that consistently lead the business cycle by at least a few months. The current leading indicators are:

1. Number of hours in the average workweek. Changing the hours of work for existing employees is a first step before changing the number of employed persons. The measurement is average workweek, production workers in manufacturing.

2. Number of initial claims for unemployment insurance. First claims by the newly unemployed forecast subsequent unemployment down the road. Measured in average weekly initial claims, state unemployment insurance (thousands).

3. Volume of manufacturers' new orders. New orders precede final sales to consumers. Measured in manufacturers' new orders, consumer goods, and materials (1992 $mil.).

4. Manufacturers' new orders, nondefense capital goods (1992 $mil.).

5. Vendor performance. Slower deliveries of raw materials may indicate greater sales of raw materials and subsequent greater sales of finished goods. Measured by slower deliveries diffusion index (percent).

6. New building permits. Housing construction begins with permits to build. Measured in number of building permits (thousands).

7. Stock market prices. Stock prices reflect the market's consensus of expected economic activity in the future. When the market moves up, the economy is expected to improve. Measured in stock prices. Standard & Poor's 500-stock index covers 500 common stocks.

8. The money supply. Monetary expansions and contractions are known to precede overall economic expansions and contractions due to the lag in the effect of monetary policy. Measured in money supply, M2 (1992 $bil.).

Inflation: How It Affects Your Business

Inflation is an increase in prices, and the inflation rate is the percent rise in those prices. Deflation is a decrease in prices, while disinflation is a slow-down in the rate of price increases. For the operations manager, as for the marketing and financial managers, a rise in the inflation rate should forewarn a decrease in demand for nonessential services and goods.

For example, an apple (representing a fixed income) can be cut in two pieces. If one piece becomes bigger (nondiscretionary purchases under infla-tion and fixed income), the second piece necessarily becomes smaller. This is further aggravated by increased prices: Since each purchase takes a bigger bite out of the whole, the consumer will be able to make fewer purchases. This is because of the inversely proportional relationship of the consumer's purchases of essential to nonessential services and goods, given a fixed personal income. Thus, wage controls without price controls (or transfer payments like Social Security or food stamps) that fail to rise at a rate consistent with that of infla-tion is indeed a cruel policy.

However, if the apple is allowed to expand at the same rate as the bites, there is no relative change. In this case, inflation would have little effect other than a devaluation of the currency in real terms. Unfortunately, inflation rarely (if ever) affects all sectors of the economy equally. Some industries (for example, oil products-based manufacturing in 1974) are crippled by rising prices in certain commodities. No business is affected by inflation in exactly the same way. Think of dropping stones (representing changes in prices) into a river (representing the U.S. economy). Since these stones vary in their size and location, the cumulative effect of the ripples (a company's individual vul-nerability to all of the individual changes in prices) will depend upon the company's size and proximity to the stones and the way in which the ripples interact. Therefore, every business owner must determine the business's own susceptibility to inflation.

Business managers should therefore interpret inflation rates as a lawyer might interpret "general rules" and look to specific shocks as "exceptions." A rising inflation rate generally points to a reduction in consumer purchases of discretionary services and products. The operations manager of firms in such industries needs to scale back production. The marketing manager needs to look for ways to make the product more desirable to the consumer, either by changing the product features, by lowering the purchase price, or by extend-ing credit. The financial manager can count on paying a higher "rent" for the use of investors' money. In periods of inflation, the investor will demand a higher than usual rate of return for long-term investments, since the

Before you make plans based on megatrends, take a closer look at your local economy. One business researcher set out to study the Milwaukee economy, beginning with the state's employment-security records—the payroll and employment data filed by every company as part of the unemployment insurance system. At the regional level, the picture looked relatively simple. Looking closer, local trends were apparent. Milwaukee had lost a torrent of factory jobs, with one-third of manufacturing employment vanishing. Suburban Milwaukee County was hit almost as hard. But wait! Waukesha County, just west of the city, added nearly 4,000 manufacturing jobs on top of an already sizable industrial base.

Business-to-business suppliers thrive by pinpointing booming markets. How many knew that one Milwaukee-area county was growing at a rate rivaling southern California in the late 1980s? The data showed which industries were creating the new jobs, which led to pinpointing the exact companies. In this way, local trends could be shown that were not apparent in the regional economic snapshot. Any company doing business locally will be as much concerned with local trends as with the national economic picture.

---

investment will be paid back with dollars worth less than those invested. As before, the financial manager should consider turning his or her attention toward short-term markets to meet capital needs during inflation.

During deflation, the consumer can purchase more goods with a given personal income. The production manager needs to start ensuring that various ingredients for production will be available for increased output. The marketing manager faces a dilemma: The value the business receives for goods or services is less than that under previous stable prices. Should prices be raised while competitors' prices may be falling? Market share would fall dramatically, as would sales revenues. The financial manager would start howling. At the same time that revenues would be dropping, each dollar taken in from sales would be worth less, creating a need for more and more sources of capital. The only saving grace would be that the firm's purchases would cost less, reducing the total amount of capital needed for the firm's production.

And here is where the error in the analogy of an apple as fixed personal income becomes glaringly apparent. Personal income cannot remain constant during periods of inflation and deflation, given stable employment. Not only does inflation determine the size of the slices, it greatly contributes to the size of the pie (GDP) as well. Now, to make things more complex, suppose that the unemployment rate fluctuates. With a high real GDP, firms will need more production workers. Unemployment will drop, but wages will rise. This expense will be passed on in the form of higher prices to the consumer and will fuel inflation. On the other hand, low real GDP would reduce the need for workers, raising the unemployment rate while slowing inflation. Thus, the user of forecasts of macroeconomic variables must also consider the interaction of economic variables.

Sampling the Sources of Economic Data

Forecasts of the five major macroeconomic variables (inflation, unemployment, GDP, interest rates, and foreign exchange rates) are available from commercial forecasting services, government agencies, and major business publications such as *The Wall Street Journal*.

Not surprisingly, the federal government is a prolific source of such data. Much government analysis is available on the World Wide Web. Every state in the Union has a home page linking to economic data. The Federal Reserve Banks have Web sites. Many statistics are available through the U.S. Congress and the White House. Monthly indicators are prepared and published monthly for the Joint Economic Committee by the Council of Economic Advisers. They can be searched on the Web at www.access.gpo.gov/congress/cong002.html. Through the GPO Access service of the Government Printing Office, in Washington, D.C., full-text databases are available. A Web page offering these monthly reports is at www.gpo.ucop.edu/info/econind.html.

Another Web resource is the Economic Statistics Briefing Room (ESBR), at www.whitehouse.gov/fsbr/esbr.html. According to the ESBR home page, "The purpose of this service is to provide easy access to current federal economic indicators. It provides links to information produced by a number of federal agencies. All of the information included in the Economic Statistics Briefing Room is maintained and updated by the statistical units of those agencies." Also on the Web is the Census Economic Briefing Room, which crunches 14 different indicators at www.census.gov/briefrm/esbr/www/brief.html.

Another resource is the wealth of government documents deposited at your local library. Look especially for the *Economic Report of the President*. Published each February, the report presents detailed, annualized data in tables updated through the end of the previous calendar year. More detailed information on specific aspects of the national economy can be obtained by contacting the appropriate federal bureau, such as the Bureau of Labor

Statistics, the Board of Governors of the Federal Reserve System, or the Federal Reserve Bank nearest you.

The business magazines piled high in your office often present summary economic information. Most business publications (such as *Inc.* magazine, *Business Week, Fortune, Forbes, The Economist, Money,* and *Time*) offer commentary by economics experts. Radio and television news broadcasts, particularly business broadcast outlets such as CNBC, provide up-to-date economic reporting, summarized for general audiences with a business bent.

Finally, the 12 regional banks of the Federal Reserve System (Atlanta, Boston, Chicago, Cleveland, Dallas, Kansas City, Minneapolis, New York, Philadelphia, Richmond, St. Louis, and San Francisco) publish a variety of reviews and quarterlies. Most are available free. Each region also has a Web site. At the national level, the monthly *Federal Reserve Bulletin* can be ordered from the Board of Governors and the U.S. Government Printing Office (Washington, D.C. 20402, Attention: Superintendent of Documents). These resources offer data needed to construct your own macroeconomic forecasts, as well as the latest academic research and professional thinking on the subject.

Summary

Forecasting the economy is an important part of business planning. If you have sound notions about what's going to happen in the future, you can plan ahead to maximize the use of borrowed funds, gauge production to meet your customers' demands, and make the most of new markets, new sources of labor, and new product lines.

Economic forecasts are now easily available through many channels. The Internet and business media have popularized economics as a way of relating businesses to the world at large. Trends can also be forecast on a smaller scale, such as by industry or region. If you are involved in your business's finances, then economic forecasting will be your partner in planning the right long-term and short-term moves.

Action Plan

Using Economic Forecasts

❏ Monitor forecasts of the five major macroeconomic variables: inflation, unemployment, GDP, interest rates, and foreign exchange rates.

❏ Assess the implications of these forecasts on your company's operations, marketing, and finance.

CHAPTER 4

Financing Your Business

Financing a business is a simple enough concept: You must have adequate funds to enable your business to start, expand, and continue operations. The needs are different between a start-up and a growing/maturing company. And the purpose of the financing—e.g., short-term vs. long-term—helps determine where the financing comes from.

The purpose of this topic is to explain the various types of financing needed for different purposes by most small businesses. We will also identify likely sources of these funds. You must know how much you need of each type before you can start looking for places to get it.

Understanding the types and sources of financing will help you to avoid the four most common abuses of business funds:

1. Undercapitalization
2. Excess debt
3. Insufficient use of credit
4. "Friday night" financing

Small businesses are almost always undercapitalized or thinly capitalized. They are much more susceptible to the negative impact of a substantial mistake than larger organizations, which have the financial resources to absorb more than one major error.

Financing must not take place apart from other aspects of your operation or separate from your business plan. In fact, financing is the heartbeat of your operation and your business plan. It keeps the enterprise alive.

Small businesses have few fixed points by which to measure progress. Your financial plan provides one of the best benchmarks possible. Financing plans are expressed in dollars. Operations can be measured in dollars—then compared against the plan.

Remember that there are two parties involved in any financing effort: the business seeking the financing and the financier. This is important to keep in mind, because all too often a giant communication problem develops between the small business's principals and its financing sources. You can avoid such problems.

Bankers and those who handle other people's money are obliged, both legally and morally, to protect their depositors' money—their depositors take precedence over you, the borrower. A bank is not allowed to take high risks. While your business ideas may sound wonderful and attractive, a bank must place the funds of its depositors into reasonably safe and secured investments or run afoul of a stringent body of laws. All lenders must ask: "How will this loan be repaid?" If there is no clear answer to this question, then the loan should not be made.

Identify Specific Needs for Funds

If you are starting a business, you can probably list the greater portion of capital assets you will need. Included in such a list could be store fixtures, start-up costs of lease deposits, delivery equipment, office machinery and furniture, operating equipment, and real estate.

Picture your business. Spread it out like a photograph in your mind's eye. The assets that will be the basis of your business, the fixed assets, are the capital assets. While they will be described on your balance sheet in dollar terms, they are, essentially, physical items. Some intangibles may creep in, such as copyrights and patents, but the physical plant and related equipment are the first part of the business to understand.

Notice that no dollars have yet entered the considerations. The needs come first, then their timing and duration. For example: You have an ongoing need for a place to do business, say, a factory if you're a manufacturer. Then you need equipment to make whatever your product is—drill presses, turret lathes, tools to keep them going, and so forth. You also need materials—but here the need is of a different duration. You buy material, use it up in a short period, sell the finished product, buy more material, and so on. You have begun to enter the realm of current assets. And the ways to finance current assets are different.

Unhappily, most people go from "Let me see how much I can raise..." to "What will I do with the money?" and never address themselves to the basic question: *"What business needs must be met?"* Ignoring this is one reason so many small businesses fail. Identify the needs, then—if you cannot finance the resolution of those needs properly—decide what to do. Don't jump in before you know what you're jumping into or you'll go broke.

Capital assets are expected to be paid for principally from invested capital, secondarily from the proceeds of long-term loans. *It is important to tie debt life to asset life.* Short-term needs should be covered by short-term debt. Long-term or capital needs should be covered by long-term debt or invested capital.

How Much Money Is Needed?

The triple approach of high/low/most-likely works well here. For every contemplated purchase or investment, cost a range that reflects what you would buy if on an unlimited budget, what you would buy if on a survival budget, and the most likely figure: one that is somewhat above survival but well below extravagance.

To arrive at a rough approximation of your capital needs, you must calculate the following:

1. *Your capital asset costs.* Plant, equipment, supplies, materials, opening inventories, perhaps other costs as well if they are capitalized.

2. *The deepest (largest) negative cash flow.* This is found only by pushing a cash flow projection out far enough to be sure that you will have adequate operating positive cash flow to carry on normal business operations. This will be a particularly important exercise if you are entering a period of sharp growth. (See Chapter 7 for more on cash management.)

3. *A safety margin.* Your accountant can help with all of these, but you must be the one to provide the insight into your business.

Then, add 1, 2, and 3. This will give you a rough total of the capital you need. If anything, it will call for more capital than is absolutely necessary. Fine, you can adjust later—but the added safety factor represented by overcapitalization helps you sleep nights. You won't kill your business by having too much capital. You might kill it, eventually, by having too little.

The other approach is for all other financing purposes. Begin by identifying the needs, then place high, low, and most likely costs against those needs. This is one of the times to ask, once again, the basic question: *"Do we really need this?"* If the need stands up and the dollar cost is not out of reach, then you are in position once again to know, not merely guess, how much money you must raise.

This is another danger point. All too often the glittering spectacle of acquiring a new toy outweighs prudence. Make sure that the acquisition (whether of a thing or a service or a skill) will be justified in terms of achieving your business's objectives. By knowing how much it will cost, you have a partial handle on this judgment. Without planning, you'll end up with enough debt to get you in trouble but not enough credit to get you out again.

What Kind of Money Is Needed?

The second most common financing error (following undercapitalization) is securing the wrong kind of financing. The variety of ways to do this is almost endless.

If the purpose of a loan is seasonal, it must be paid off seasonally. If it is stretched out to a long-term loan, then the next year the same problem will get worse. The parallel here is to consumer debt: Waldo gets behind on his monthly bills, so he gets a debt consolidation loan. He now spreads repayment of short-term debt needs over a long term; this makes his cash flow look pretty good until he gets deeper into debt (he hasn't changed the consumption pattern that got him in this bind in the first place). So he has to reconsolidate. And re-reconsolidate. And so forth. The hole just gets deeper and deeper, and the monthly payments get bigger and bigger.

A business is no different. Recurrent loan needs are best handled by a financing vehicle designed for that kind of need.

The other side of this coin is trying to finance long-term needs, say, for fixed asset acquisition, over a short term by abusing a nonrevolving line of credit. This will drain off working capital with gruesome haste and can make growth impossible. It is also likely to destroy your reputation for paying your bills and servicing your debt. If you expect to use that expensive turret lathe for the next 10 years, then don't try to pay for it in six months. A term loan for 4 years or so might be the best way to go.

Whether the need is for debt or capital, you must consider the cost. One reason for the repeated warning against carrying too much debt is that the cost of that money—the interest and the principal repayment—may exceed the return you can earn after expenses on that money. This is a fine way to slowly go broke, almost painless until suddenly there's no working capital (except illiquid receivables) and no credit.

High debt-to-worth ratios (high leverage) can show spectacular returns on invested capital. But if things don't work out—and they seldom do (the best laid plans...) then the loss figures are also spectacular, and net worth vanishes.

Too little capital will rapidly surface as negative net worth—and the only remedy for negative net worth is new investment. In most cases, financing sources are wary of lending into a negative net worth situation. Would you want to invest in a company whose management lacked the basic foresight to properly capitalize its business—and then ran it at a loss to boot? Of course not. Yet that is exactly what many borrowers expect lenders to do!

Figure the cost. If you usually net 5% on gross sales and debt costs your company 15% to 18%, then that cost must be justified in terms of increased sales, increased efficiency, greater profits, or all three. Otherwise it merely becomes an added burden. One excellent safeguard for retailers is found in the sales/worth ratio. If your sales/worth ratio is higher than trade averages, then you're overtrading—making a small amount of capital work overtime. This is a risky disease. The cure is more capital—not more debt.

Your banker and accountant can help you here. You will be doubly protected, however, by looking for what kind of financing makes the most sense for you, both now and in the long run, before you go to your financing sources. Expedience will hurt you. Take a relatively conservative path, and you'll do yourself and your investors a favor.

Credit and debt, properly used, enable you to grow faster than an ultra-conservative no-debt strategy. Not to use financing is about as sane as playing baseball without going up to bat—pure defensiveness is ultimately self-defeating. There's a middle course between excessive debt and ultraconservatism that's difficult to steer. It all starts by identifying legitimate business needs.

When Is It Needed?

Identify the timing. Plan ahead and set specific dates. A common error in small-business circles is to leave financing needs until the last moment, the moment at which they become so pressing that a slight hitch in securing financing can seriously damage the business.

Once you know what kind of money and how much money is needed, then, and only then, can you start setting up a timetable. For example: A line of credit for a new company may take several months to be approved and in place, whereas a well-established company might get the same line for the same purposes over the phone. A real estate deal will almost always take four weeks or longer; the legalities alone make that a sure bet. A term loan may have to wait for an evaluation of the equipment being financed. A construction or a progress loan will have a built-in timetable but will never take less than several weeks to negotiate. Visit your banker well before you need to and ask for the timing on the kind of loan you may need. Your banker will happily tell you. So will your accountant. By seeing your banker before you desperately need help, you avoid the "Friday night" financing problem.

If you know that added capital for growth is going to be needed in a year and that capital will not be generated from operating profits, start hunting up new capital now, before you panic. Investors need time—and if that puts you in a hard place, you'll either not get the financing or the financing will be more costly (in terms of equity, control, or interest) than it needs to be.

Develop a Financing Plan

Part of your strategy should be to make sure that you and your financing prospects keep in touch during lean times as well as prosperous times. Get your financiers to visit your place. This gives them a feel for your business in a physical way, gives you the home-court advantage, and even lets them offer suggestions. This kind of advice can be tremendously helpful.

Case: Bank Borrowing Should "Jell in a Week"

Patrick Toth, owner of Kansas Quick Lube, in Colby, Kans., recently obtained approximately $550,000 in financing for his new business. From his experience, he says, "If it's not jelling in a week, maybe you're not working with the right lender."

While qualifying for favorable terms, Toth was repeatedly stymied in his efforts to move beyond the initial financing phase of his business. "Every day is a day—a day to build a customer base, a day to develop a reputation, a day to gain experience. If you're working with the wrong institution, it doesn't matter how long it takes. There's always going to be one more hurdle to cross."

Toth found this out the hard way by going through a never-ending process with several institutions successively, always being asked to provide one more document or one more guarantee. Then he came in contact with a bank that reviewed his application and tentatively approved his loan within a week, contingent upon appraisals and surveys. He considers timing to be very important and says he has learned that "if you work with the right lender, it should take about a week."

Your financing proposal will vary with your relationship to your sources of financing. If you are well established, you will need no more than updated financial statements and a statement of intended use and source of repayment of your debt. For a new or rapidly growing business, you'll need a more comprehensive plan, which should be updated periodically whether you need more outside financing or not. A good plan is a lot of work and will take a lot of time, but the benefits are guaranteed to far outweigh these considerations.

Your aim should be to keep your sources of financing favorably aware of your progress toward clearly defined business objectives. In a word: credibility. A banker's aim is protection of depositors' money. The banker's prime concern: How will the loan be repaid? The investor's aim is to achieve either a satisfactory percentage return on capital investment or to achieve a good capital gain, or both. Honesty with your banker and other financiers is not just the best policy; it's the only policy.

Everyone—including your other financing sources—wants to earn a return on his or her money that is in line with the amount of risk. Ordinarily, a low risk investment isn't expected to generate as high returns as a high risk investment. The best financing sources are those who are familiar with your type of business. Keep the source of the money in mind as you prepare the initial proposal. Also keep in mind that your plan may not succeed with the first source, or even the second. But, if it's a good plan, it will find the necessary combination of debt and equity financing.

You might also want to form two contrasting strategies: a capital-conservative plan and a more highly leveraged plan. If you could bootstrap your business, but it would pinch your growth, putting the two plans side-by-side will almost always encourage your banker to give you the credit you need for maximum safe growth. Good financial planning is a key indicator of managerial competence.

Implement and Review

Securing and applying the financing is only the beginning. While a bad financing decision will have long-lasting and deep-rooted effects, good plans can degrade into poor plans unless they are reviewed and recast periodically. Don't hang onto last year's plans too long, because time brings change. Habits form all too easily—in business financing, as well as in other areas.

Do enough planning to make sure you don't botch the financing—either by not getting it or by the all-too-human process of mistaking securing a loan for business success. This often happens: A business secures a medium-term loan for working capital purposes (a legitimate and appropriate use of debt), but the owner promptly goes out and buys a few goodies for the business, forgetting about the working capital needs. A bloated cash supply must be checked by a written plan of what to do with the loan proceeds. Don't fall victim to this kind of error. You made your plan based on purely business considerations; follow it.

Since your financing needs are ongoing (if you stay in business and aren't ultraconservative, the odds are you'll use trade credit and bank financing on a regular basis), your plan should be reviewed at least annually—preferably more often. There is a built-in bonus in all this. Once formulated, your financing plan becomes an integral part of your budget/control process. Used in this manner, you will be tuned to the need for both positive and negative changes on a regular basis, and you'll be able to respond to these needs to your maximum benefit.

Summary

By carefully analyzing your financing needs and expressing them in an objective way, you avoid problems caused by inadequate capitalization, excessive debt, poor use of the powerful tool of credit (both trade and other debt), and "Friday night" financing attempts that either fail or make you fail. Good financial management follows from a clear understanding of how and why money takes different shapes and fills different purposes in your business—and good financial management leads to a better and more profitable business.

Action Plan

Financing

❏ Identify different needs for funds within the business. What needs require cash from outside the business? What can be financed from operations? What will be financed?

❏ Determine how much money is needed. Be specific.

❏ Decide what kind of money is needed: debt or new capital; short term or long term; permanent capital or temporary debt.

❏ Determine ahead of time when you need the money.

❏ Develop a financing plan to anticipate and answer your bankers' or other investors' questions. Go over your plan with them; solicit and respond to their ideas and advice.

❏ Implement your financial plan. Review it as needed, at least annually if not more often.

CHAPTER 5

Debt Management and Banking

W hat levels of debt can your business safely support? Can you control the amount, timing, and availability of credit? That is, can you ensure the timely inflow of cash from new debt?

Assume that you have done all you can realistically do to control your cash flow, but you still face occasional periods of cash shortfalls. To tide you over these periods, you have to borrow from a commercial bank. How do you go about preparing a financing proposal? This chapter is intended to help you understand and deal with your banker as an equal. Its five steps follow from basic cash flow controls (see Chapters 6 and 7). Unless your cash flow is already under control, additional financing is unwise.

Focus on Receivables, Collection, and Inventory

Your largest current assets, against which you might borrow, are probably receivables and inventory. Ideally, both of these assets turn into cash as soon as you wish. However, unless you manage them carefully, they tend to become a problem. To manage your working capital properly, you must know:

1. The age of your receivables and inventory,
2. The turn of your receivables and inventory, and
3. The concentration of your receivables (how many customers comprise the majority of your receivables, what amount of receivables they represent,

what products the receivables cover) and inventory by product lines.

You must also know what your credit and collection policies are doing to your working capital. All too often small-business owners mistake sales for profits. They extend more and more credit, pursue lax collection policies, and end up financing their customers to increase sales. Most businesses cannot afford to provide interest-free loans to customers just because they expect it. Slow-paying customers must be subjected to profitability analysis, which takes in their carrying costs. If sales increases don't translate into profits on the bottom line, then you are buying trouble faster than you are increasing profits by carrying customers who habitually stretch their payments.

Receivables Management

To control receivables, begin by examining their age. Break receivables out weekly to spot the slow-pay accounts as soon as possible. Then you can try to collect before the accounts cost you your profits.

Aging receivables is simple: Separate invoices into Current, 30 days, 60 days, 90 days, and more than 90 days. Then figure out your collection period: Divide annual credit sales by 365 to find the average daily credit sale. Next, divide your current outstanding receivables total by the average daily credit sale. This yields your collection period.

Here's a good rule of thumb for a quick test of your receivables management: If your collection period is more than one third greater than your credit terms (for example, 40 days if your terms are net 30), you have a looming problem.

Credit and Collection

The cost of extending credit is one of those hidden costs that eats up working capital. Most of us aren't credit experts; we grant credit terms because others do, and we fail to understand what we are doing. Very few smaller businesses have explicit credit policies. If they did, they could dramatically increase both profits and the quality of their current assets.

You should investigate the possible use of credit cards. These cost little in return for the headaches they save you. Consider the cost, in direct bad debt losses, and in time, effort and attention that slow-pay accounts cost you. The added costs of capital tied up in receivables, for example, is frequently greater than the fee charged by the major credit card companies.

Follow-Up Form

Collections

Name: _____

Telephone: _____

Spoke to: _____

Title: _____

Subject: _____

Date: _____

Time: _____

Initials: _____

☐ No answer
☐ Requested info
☐ Order never received
☐ Will send check
☐ Duplicate billing

☐ Not available
☐ Requested proof of delivery
☐ Payment previously sent
☐ Merchandise returned
☐ Payment being held

Comments: _____

Returned call: _____

Follow-up: _____

Use the form on page 45 every time you call a lagging account. It provides back-up information if you turn the account over to a collection agency or have to prosecute the matter in court. The completed slip should be filed for reference on further calls. Remember to ask for specific payments on specific dates. If payment is not received, call back and ask again.

Managing Your Inventory

Inventory management, like receivables management, is often overlooked as a source of operating profits. Careful attention to how you manage these two areas can often spring cash and improve operating profits without recourse to bank borrowing. If you are managing both of these areas well, congratulate yourself—you are in a distinct minority.

Carrying costs of inventory can run as high as 30% of average inventory, a substantial drain on working capital. Consider the costs of storage, spoilage, pilferage, inventory loans, and so on. They add up fast.

Determining the right level of inventory to carry is a difficult problem. On the one hand you want to avoid unnecessary expenses, while on the other you want to avoid as many stock-outs as possible. Trying to manage inventory on a day-to-day basis invites trouble; accordingly, most businesses use some kind of inventory policy.

The three most important factors in deciding on an inventory policy are *inventory turn* (how many times per year, and how does that compare with other businesses in the same line?), *reorder time* (planning on a 10-day reorder time is vastly different from a 210-day reorder), and who your *suppliers* are.

Inventory control is a balancing act. If your inventory gets too high, you run out of cash. If it is too low, the chances are excellent that either you are buying in uneconomical quantities (a danger sign to bankers), are too under-capitalized to ever become profitable (another danger sign), or are bleeding the business. Bankers are increasingly interested in the quality of inventory as well as the more standard indicators of good management (liquidity, profitability, and track record). If you have a cogent inventory policy and follow it, you will upgrade both inventory quality and profitability.

Establish a Contingency Plan

A contingency plan is a plan you hope never to use: It outlines what you would do if all of your optimistic plans went wrong. It doesn't have to be lengthy. In some cases, it can be as short as a single page and still be more than adequate, although for most businesses it will be somewhat longer.

A contingency plan should provide answers to the following questions:

1. What suppliers would give you extended terms or carry you in case of a crunch? Why would they carry you? How long, and how much?
2. What new investment could you make? Would you refinance personal assets to provide a cash cushion for your business? Could you? What other assets could you bring to support a cash crunch?
3. What assets does your business have to either sell or turn to cash (perhaps a sale/leaseback) some other way if necessary?
4. How will you keep your banker and major trade creditors on your side?
5. Have you examined all possible sources of additional working capital in your business? Where might you have some leverage?
6. What customers would be willing to prepay or speed up orders if it would help you?

The purpose of a contingency plan is to make sure before a crisis is at hand that you won't panic. As evidence of thoughtful business management, it's hard to beat and is being sought by more and more creditors.

Incidentally, the purpose of collateralizing a loan (for small business, this usually means pledging personal assets to support a business loan) is not to make the bank a secondhand asset dealer but to tie you more closely to the business. If all the assets at stake belong to the bank and times get tough, you might be tempted to let go sooner than if your own assets were at stake.

Tighten and Maintain Cash Controls

Cash flow control begins with the cash flow budget. If you don't have a cash flow budget, you will have cash flow problems.

You also need a sales budget or its equivalent to keep the sales level where it should be. Small sales lags can add up to big problems if not spotted early—ranging from a less than honest clerk to a sluggish salesperson.

Your cash flow budget is a tool for keeping overhead costs down. You have a degree of control over costs that you don't have over sales; while you can almost always cut costs, you can't generate sales (especially cash sales) whenever you need to. If you could, you'd never have a cash flow problem and would not need financing.

Every budget has some fat in it. Tightening controls means always asking whether this or that purchase or expenditure will have a positive effect on your business. If there is no clear answer, examine the expenditure closely. This effort must be consistent to work. All the controls in the book will do you no good unless they are applied—whether the control is a separation of purchasing from paying, making sure that bills and reorders go out when they should, or even keeping a physical count of the inventory.

Determine Your Financing Needs

At some point, no matter how carefully you monitor your cash flow, you will have to borrow money from a bank. There are two main reasons to borrow: to cover a temporary cash flow gap and to provide working capital for the growth of your business.

Plan ahead. A written financing plan—whether for bank or internal use—is a major step in the right direction. A financing plan helps you avoid the causes of cash flow problems, anticipate financing needs (for growth or for survival), and helps keep your total borrowing under control.

A financing plan spells out detailed responses to such questions as: What are the needs? Why can't they be met from retained earnings? Are operating profits going to be available to meet long-term debt? How much is needed, when, and under what terms? Most important, the plan should provide an answer to the banker's biggest question: How will this loan be repaid?

You must be able to show that you can afford to service the loan. One of the classic ways small businesses trip themselves up is to use this year's financing to pay off last year's debt. This pyramiding is doubly defeating. It creates a larger debt load than is wise, and it is very discouraging to be always behind the eight-ball even while the profitability is going up. Be wary of using financing to conceal operating losses.

How do you put together a financing plan? Start by identifying the different needs for funds. Most of these will be covered by operating profits. Those that cannot be (or cannot without making the liquidity vanish) should be carefully analyzed to see whether more debt should be sought.

The important thing to keep in mind is that if debt financing is needed to cover a cash flow gap ordinarily caused by insufficient operating profits, the underlying cause must be identified and dealt with before financing will do any good. Borrowing to paper over an operating problem always leads to a worsened situation, tempting though it may be at the time.

Suppose, for example, that your sales have fallen off and costs have risen, making it clear that soon you will have a severe liquidity or working capital problem. If the lag in sales can be cured without borrowing, fine. (You can almost always take costs down a few notches.) If you will still have a cash flow problem, then make sure that the borrowing won't make it worse. If the sales problem can't be resolved, sooner or later you'll be back to the bank to borrow more, thus driving costs even higher.

Make sure you know your needs before going to the bank—both in dollar terms and in what benefits that cash inflow will have. Any banker you'd want to work with will ask what you need the money for and whether you could raise it from operations. To stammer and admit you haven't looked for operating economies and profits as a way to generate money is a sure way to lose credibility. Avoid this. Enter the bank well prepared.

Legitimate financing needs fall into five related categories. At any one time you may need to use several of these. A start-up, for example, may include radical expansion, perhaps by acquisition or by starting up a new division.

1. *Start-ups.* A new business needs a combination of investment capital and long-term debt. One error that cripples a lot of small businesses is the use of short-term debt to finance long-term needs. The basic rule in financing is to match the term of the loan to both the term of the need and to the source of repayment. Using a 90-day note for permanent financing needs is very risky. Not only is there the ever-present danger that the loan will not be renewed (bank examiners frown on "evergreen" notes), but there is the added disadvantage of never being able to plan more than 90 days ahead.

2. *Working capital shortages.* After initial capitalization, working capital should be generated from operating profits over a long period. If you suffer from chronic working capital shortages due to undercapitalization but are making some operating profits, then the answer may be a term loan if you can demonstrate that the loan will more than repay itself in additional operating profits. Sometimes a modest working capital loan will put a business over the hump, affording enough breathing room to make much higher operating profits.

But remember: A working capital loan, which is paid back monthly over a period of three to seven years, adds to the basic nut. If your business won't generate sufficient operating profits to cover the payments comfortably, then added equity is needed, not another loan.

3. *Equipment and other fixed assets.* Equipment and other fixed-asset loans are about the clearest example of matching a loan to the need and payment base. Since these loans are ordinarily secured by the equipment, the anticipated useful life of the equipment becomes a major factor in the credit decision. A rough guideline is that you can finance equipment with a projected useful life of 10 years for up to 70% of its life and for as much as 90% of its value.

Don't buy fixed assets on 90-day notes. The timing is wrong. If you are trying to make your business work on sweat equity, you may want to go ahead and pay off a piece of equipment more rapidly than we'd recommend. That's an option, but a hard one to live with.

If your banker won't visit your place of business, you aren't getting the treatment you deserve. If your banker doesn't network for you, show you how to save costs, and treat you with the respect any customer deserves, you should consider finding another bank.

Banks are going to ever-greater lengths to keep small-business customers happy. Consider the case of Randy Rolston, CEO of Victorian Papers, a $5-million mail-order catalog and two-time *Inc.* 500 company in Kansas City, Mo. When Rolston complained to his banker that he was being eaten alive by the 12¢ to 20¢ handling charges on each of the 300 to 400 checks his business was processing daily, his bank suggested a money-market account that enables him to write and process checks for free. Rolston's savings? From $60 to $70 a day.

Remarkable as it sounds, some banks don't wait for customers to complain or ask for things; instead, they anticipate their clients' needs. Carole Petranovich, CEO of Computer Corner, a $5-million computer retailer and service provider in Albuquerque that is also an *Inc.* 500 company, loves the fact that her bank does "collection services for me over and above the call of duty." Not only does it alert her to bounced checks from her customers, it calls the customer's bank on those checks, finds out if money is available, and then advises her what to do.

Laurie Snyder is pleased that her new bank, which is owned by a Japanese conglomerate, is putting her in contact with trading companies in Japan, where she is now doing some export business for her *Inc.* 500 children's clothing company, Flap Happy, in Santa Monica, Calif. After shopping around at 10 banks, Snyder chose her new bank because "they're always asking me what more they can do for me."

Entrepreneurs cite many other ways in which banks are meeting their needs. For example, some bankers offer lessons in online banking or reading financial statements. Others invite clients and prospective clients to educational seminars and community events. Still others serve as an informal board of directors for their small-business clients.

Service is one reason to switch banks. Another is that the premiums of staying with a bank and building a long-term relationship are vanishing in today's volatile marketplace. A bank might want your business one day and then change its mind the next. Moral: Always have at least two banks.

While equipment loans rarely go beyond 7 years, commercial real estate may be financed over 10 or more years, depending on the situation. Since you are building equity in equipment and real estate over a number of years from profits, you should finance it the same way.

4. *Inventory, seasonal progress.* These loans are short-term and usually are tied to a clearly defined source of repayment, such as one inventory turn, fulfillment of a contract, or sale of a specific asset.

Short-term notes are repaid from short-term sources, clearly identified before the credit is granted. Medium- and long-term debts, on the other hand, are repaid from more indirect sources. A banker looks to proven management ability (usually evidenced by a profitable history and clearly understood plans) for repayment. Since there is no single fast source of repayment, the risk is greater and the decision more difficult. This is a crucial distinction. A poorly run company may be an excellent short-term credit risk, but for long-term credit, a business must demonstrate ability to consistently generate profits.

Remember, term loans come due every month, adding to the nut. As the nut gets bigger, so does the risk and the need for more careful management.

5. *Sustained growth.* The final major category of bankable loans is for growth, which can outstrip working capital. A business anticipating fast growth can also anticipate a lot of danger. As sales go up, liquidity goes down, creating a heightened threat of insolvency. A combination of investment, lines of credit tied to receivables and inventory, and long-term working capital loans is the normal answer.

Notice what this implies. If you plan to grow, you must plan to generate profits consistently, at the same time keeping your business liquid to meet current obligations. To make sure that you maintain liquidity, you have to make sure of your financing. The answer? A financing plan.

Work with Your Banker

If you aren't comfortable preparing a financing proposal complete with financial statements, or if you feel that your banking relationships could be improved, get your banker involved in your long-term planning efforts.

Bankers are like everyone else—they like to use their skills. Since most businesses suffer from a lack of financial management skills, and since most bankers have these skills, it is to your advantage to make the first move. Invite your banker to help you.

Level with him or her. If you can't keep communications open, then you won't get help—and you will quite possibly not get the financing you need. Your banker can tell if your business is a bind. Banks are primarily information clearinghouses, and it takes little skill to recognize altered payment and supplier relations from daily and weekly bank activities.

The sooner you can get your banker on your side, the better. If your banker won't visit your place of business, you aren't getting the treatment you deserve—after all, nobody is smart enough to understand a business without actually seeing it in operation.

Summary

Debt management and cash flow management are inseparable. A poorly managed cash flow will eventually surface as a depletion of working capital. If working capital never presented a problem, you'd never have to go into debt.

Your aim is to manage cash flow to minimize debt load—and generate better profits. The right debt at the right time, under the right terms, is a powerful tool. But like any mismanaged tool, it will cause damage in direct proportion to its power.

After making sure your cash flow is under control—including receivables and inventory management—you should consider getting your banker involved in your planning. At the very least, you'll enhance your credibility; more likely, you'll find that you can turn the banker's skills into a positive resource rather than a roadblock.

Action Plan

Debt Management and Banking

❏ Focus on receivables, collection, and inventory. These can lead to an increase in cash over a short time, lessening the need to borrow.

❏ Establish a contingency plan. It prevents panic and builds valuable credibility.

❏ Tighten and maintain cash controls—continuously.

❏ Determine your financing needs. Minimize your company's borrowing needs whenever possible.

❏ Work with your banker in foul times as well as fair. Check in at least quarterly—and share the bad news as well as the good.

CHAPTER 6

Forecasting and Cash Flow Budgeting

Your financial statements operate as a kind of distant early warning system when carefully prepared and used. In the previous chapters on financing and debt management, the importance of a cash flow projection was tied not only to figuring out how much money you need, but also when you need it. The projected profit-and-loss (P&L) statement (a.k.a. income statement) helps identify how the loan will be repaid.

These statements work together. You use the P&L projection to determine profitability; this provides the basis for a detailed cash flow pro forma which in turn becomes your budget. It also is the basis for your financing plan, the best means of testing the feasibility of your business goals, and a key element in the survival of your business.

If you could have only one financial statement to guide you, it should be the cash flow budget. It is the most important financial statement you can have—it models your business; provides the necessary checks, balances, and financial controls to guide performance; wins bankers' hearts; and keeps spending and investment impulses under control.

Anyone can set a budget, but only an exceptionally good manager can set a budget that works—and that works not only as a necessary cash control, but also as a positive means to attain your business goals.

Forecasting and budgeting are closely related. Once you have made your sales and expense forecasts, the actual budgeting process is simple—but if your forecasts are out of line, your budget will not stand up to the everyday demands of your business. Sometimes only hard experience can refine the process. Preparing a budgeting system is one of the most exacting tasks you face as a business owner. The budget is the basic tool of the manager who looks to the future and prepares for what is in store.

Would you start out on a trip before deciding on a destination? Once the destination is determined, would you start off before mapping out the best route? Of course not! The same holds true for your business. The same logic that demands planning for a trip also demands a well thought-out budget. By putting your plan in writing—as you set and evaluate your goals, tactics, and strategy—you will be in the best possible position to improve your forecasting and budgeting skills *and* your company's profits.

How do you go about the daunting task of forecasting?

First, set broad guidelines and goals to be achieved during the budget period and beyond. These guidelines and goals will become more precise as your forecasting/budgeting proceeds. Don't try to start out with your goals finetuned. Second, review current business conditions and carefully examine the facts and figures pertaining to your business. You prepare your forecast or projection to assist you in determining the goals of your enterprise, but those goals must reflect reality. Be realistic. As you zero in on your precise objectives and forecasts, rethink your business practices and policies.

From Budget to Business Trends

With your goals set and strategies in mind, your budget tells you what it will take to reach your desired profit level. The road to business success is full of pitfalls and potential setbacks. How you handle these problems will be covered in the budget; at the very least, you need positive cash flow to survive. This is why you budget.

Keep one eye on the present operations of your business and the other looking out for future trends. This is not easy, especially if your business is heading in one direction while trends are pointing in the other. For example, consider the plight of the personal computer industry when it was unable to forecast demand at different price points. Margins began to erode as PC manufacturers had to lower prices on existing machines and learn to build a popular machine with a low price point. All because forecasting demand for PCs is subject to many complex factors.

To operate your business effectively, focus on the factors that affect all businesses and then keep an eye on events that will have the most direct effect on yours. Successful entrepreneurs are aware of the general business outlook and how it will affect their concerns. No forecasts are 100% accurate. However, many events that affect your business are known and can be planned for well in advance. A new shopping center, new road construction, altered bus routes, new housing developments, and similar events are proposed long before their effects are felt. Every business should have been prepared for increased payroll and FICA taxes and the health-care cost crisis. We knew these changes were coming and, therefore, we should have prepared for them.

Prepare a Profit-and-Loss Projection

The first step in your forecast is the projection of an annual profit-and-loss statement, broken down by sales and expense categories.

Your P&L projection is for a year (or for the proposed period of your budget). Since it covers a full business cycle, don't worry about seasonal fluctuations, collecting receivables, or that large reduction of an outstanding loan—you'll cover these contingencies later, when you push the cash flow projection. Don't try to break it out month by month or you'll drown in details you can't use.

This P&L projection is not intended to be a fine-tuned, fully spelled out financial statement. It is a guide, an approximation to help you arrive at an accurate forecast of sales and expenses. After you have gone through the complete budgeting process, you can make it more accurate and may wish to project a monthly or quarterly P&L for control purposes.

The first question to ask yourself is: What sales can I expect to generate in the coming months? You can answer this with the help of a profit-and-loss projection. To format your P&L projection, see page 67. You may wish to modify the format to fit your particular operation, but do not change its basic form. Used properly, this worksheet will assist you in predicting future profits.

Here are four steps to creating a profit-and-loss projection:

1. Forecast Sales

The P&L form is simple to use—what may take some doing is to let your imagination loose. During the course of the next year, what are the lowest sales figures you could expect? What are the highest? Approach the projection one step at a time.

Be reasonable. Try approaching it this way: What was your worst year recently? Your best? What was the worst single drop in sales from one period to the next? The best increase?

To forecast sales, break down your sales by product lines (or services).

Then predict the worst case and the best case, making notes on your assumptions. If you have historical sales records available, this will not be too arduous—but if your business is a start-up or in a period of rapid expansion or flux, it will be more difficult. That's understandable. But do it anyway. A rough guide to the future will help you establish more accurate guides later. You need some benchmarks to measure your progress.

Take into account normal growth patterns, inflation, and the impact of major changes in your business or industry, then establish your P&L projection for the budget period. This mode of attack helps you think in realistic terms. All you want to establish here are parameters, boundaries to think within.

The left-hand column is used to project a bare-bones profit-and-loss statement. Start by projecting sales assuming the worst conditions. If you have more than one line of goods, then project sales for each line separately. You'll want to be able to identify the losers and concentrate on your more profitable product lines.

Remember, the goal is to get a handle on the worst possible situation. Be gloomy—assume that you'll have bad weather, poor traffic, lazy salespeople. Perhaps you'll have shortages of products, disrupted delivery schedules, canceled orders. A "what-if" scenario is not meant to alarm. Sometimes it helps to take a dismal view—you may be able to identify potential soft spots in your operation. (Perhaps a competitor is going to invade your market or you won't get that contract renewal. What then?)

In the column to the right, project sales under the best possible conditions. This will be your most optimistic forecast of revenues. This is more fun. All your sales efforts will succeed, customers will beat down your door, suppliers will meet schedules so you'll never have a stock-out. Your ads will be 100% effective. This commercial utopia is about as likely to happen as the corresponding gloomy projection—but both have been known to happen.

Remember this: *80% of your profits probably come from 20% of sales.* Can you identify your winning products? Next year's winners? Declining products?

2. Forecast Expenses

Next, identify all expenses that will be incurred to generate the revenues under the low and high sales projections. The best way to gather this information is to review past operating statements and your business records. A going concern incurs expenses throughout the year. No matter what the level of production or sales, there will still be some costs. Those costs that are present and remain fairly constant at any level of output are called fixed expenses.

Expenses that increase or decrease with production are variable expenses. As sales volume increases and decreases, variable expenses increase and decrease. If there is no output, there will be no variable expenses. At zero production, only fixed expenses are incurred. For example:

Variable Costs	Fixed Costs
Cost of goods sold	Rent/mortgage payments
Cost of sales	Office expenses
Advertising	Certain taxes
Labor and sales force	Owners' salaries and withdrawals
Variable utilities	Leased equipment payments
Shop expense	Basic telephone/utilities

Each expense that your business incurs should be carefully examined. This is an education in itself. Which expenses can be justified? Which expenses can be lowered? Increased? An expense lowered by $1 with no change in sales will increase profit by the same $1. On the other hand, increasing certain expenses can often improve sales and increase profits.

As you identify all expenses as either fixed or variable, you should start to get an idea of what it takes to make your business run better. Profits get devoured by unnecessary expenses—in all businesses.

Fixed expenses will remain more or less the same under both the worst and best situations. Once you have identified which expense categories are fixed in your business, you can record the proper amount in the left- and right-hand columns. Be particularly aware of the expenses that remain constant only to a certain volume of production. For example, a payment for leased equipment may remain constant until volume requires the move to larger equipment and a higher lease payment. Fixed expenses are fixed only within broad limits; if sales go way up, you may need more salespeople, more office help, and more debt. Ramping up to meet demand can affect your fixed costs dramatically.

Variable expenses increase as sales and production increase. When projecting variable expenses, many categories will remain a constant percentage of sales. Freight, postage, cost of goods sold, and operating supplies fall into this category. For many businesses, the same holds true for telephone, laundry, and auto expenses.

Some variable expenses do not remain a constant percentage of sales. Payroll, for example, will increase only at certain sales levels. There is a minimum workforce required in most businesses. A new employee is added only when needed—that is, when production reaches the point where the present workforce is unable to keep up with demand. Payroll and payroll taxes will increase only as volume requires the increase.

In many businesses, advertising will remain a constant percentage of sales (1% or 2% of net sales, for example) to a point where the expense will level off. Or it may be necessary to make a drastic increase in advertising to take over a large share of the market.

Other expenses that fall into the uncertain variable category are utilities, repairs and maintenance, auto and truck expenses, and purchase of fixed assets. And please note that miscellaneous expense is not a catchall for those disbursements that you don't know what to do with. Suggestion: If miscellaneous expense is greater than 3% of sales, break these expenses down into smaller categories.

Don't worry too much about making the fixed/variable decision—when in doubt, consider the expense fixed. This will force a conservative forecast. For almost every small business, such conservatism is highly desirable.

3. Compare and Review "Best" and "Worst"

Once you have prepared a projected profit-and-loss statement assuming the worst and best conditions, make a comparison. In the center column of your form, prepare a projection assuming figures somewhere in between "worst" and "best." This results in a more realistic forecast.

Take the time to test your projection. Recognizing the potential and limitations of your business is critical to the success of your venture. Is the demand in the market great enough so that the desired sales level can be reached? Is your production capacity adequate to produce the desired profit level? Break down sales into units, then units per person, then units per day. Apply the test now—it will save you much time and money later.

We call this the bowl-of-soup test, after a sandwich-shop operator who needed to achieve 80% occupancy with half-hourly turnover for 10 hours a day to reach his sales goal. Since his products—soups, salads, and sandwiches—were in demand for only three hours a day, his goal was patently absurd. The final result? He expanded his menu, paid some much needed attention to cost control, and is still thriving, though with lowered goals.

4. Look at Your Profit Level

Once you have come this far, you will have three potential profit figures: one grotesquely low, one bloated—and the other, one hopes, a profit level that you and your business can live with and grow on. If the profit is not enough to cover debt retirement, then you may have to stop and rethink the business from the beginning.

This is important, yet often overlooked. One of the critical financial ratios is concerned with how many times operating profit covers debt amortization, because you'll be retiring your term debt out of operating profits. And if your profit is not high enough to comfortably cover your debt repayment, you won't stay in business long. You will also be hard-put to get additional credit of any kind.

Review all expense categories, one by one. There are some expenses that will remain hidden or overlooked, no matter how careful you are. The best way to prepare for this problem is to be conservative in your projections. You will be much better off with a slightly understated profit than to plan optimistically and fail to reach your projected profit level. Basing projections on dreams rather than the real world will only hurt you and your business.

Once again, your bottom line, net profit, must be able to support your term debt and finance a major portion of your growth. If the figure is too low, be warned. (And if it is too high, that can be a danger sign, too.)

Projection vs. Past Performance

Although no projection is 100% accurate, experience and review will make your forecasts more exact. Use your projection as a measure of your growth toward established objectives. Any large (or unusual) item entered on your projected profit-and-loss statement should be accompanied by an explanation of how you derived the figures. A simple note should suffice to remind you of how the numbers were generated.

During the comparison/review process, compare your final projection to the past performance of your business. Even though the projections (both best and worst cases) have been in part based on your actual experience, it can be a shock to first review your realistic projection the middle way. Compare it, item by item, with your historical data.

Why do this? Because experience is the great corrector of projections. No matter how carefully a projection is prepared, severe divergences from past practices need additional thought. The divergence may be justifiable—but more often it reflects wishful thinking. If the projections are radically gloomy, then you should rethink them; your goals should be realistic, not misleading or thwarting.

Where there are significant differences between projections and past practice, make notes. Later on, they'll help you understand why you made the projections differ from past practice, an understanding that is easily lost.

Preparing a Cash Flow Projection

This step has three parts and will result in a realistic cash flow budget.

1. Project your monthly cash inflows.
2. Project your monthly cash disbursements (outflows).
3. Project operating data.

Cash flow depends on dollar volume and timing. These are equally important, since cash flowing in or out of your business at the wrong time is no help at all. In the short-term, avoidable cash shortages cause panic. Long term, chronic cash shortage will surely strangle the growth of your firm or bankrupt it.

Ironically, growth is itself a major cause of cash flow problems. Not all sales are on a cash basis. You probably extend credit—and you may offer your customers more lenient terms than your suppliers offer you. Most small businesses aren't set up to pursue formal collection procedures on slow-paying accounts, so the upshot is that as you increase your sales and receivables, you run out of cash and/or trade credit. Your cash flow budget can prevent such problems.

Or suppose that your business hits a slump—a period when even your best customers are temporarily overstocked or don't need your services. For seasonal businesses, this can be disastrous. Reduced sales mean reduced cash inflow, while your fixed payments go on at their usual brisk clip. The result? Cash outflow exceeds inflow, and you go broke.

Whatever the cause of a cash flow problem, the result is the same: If you run out of cash, you run into trouble. Getting out of a cash flow problem may be impossible—yet in almost every case, the problem could have been avoided in the first place. How? By preparing a cash flow budget, following it, and revising or straying from its bounds only when you have compelling reasons. The form on pages 68 and 69 is a format we suggest for small-business use. Feel free to modify it. You'll find it covers most items. Don't omit any details peculiar to your business, though. If, for instance, you have heavy shipping costs, make an entry for it.

1. Project Your Monthly Cash Inflows

The hardest part has been done. Your projected P&L for the budget period established realistic sales levels; now the task is limited to parceling those totals over the months. It is not likely that your sales are spread evenly throughout the year, with one-twelfth of the annual sales falling in each month.

Build in seasonal variations, month by month. If all of your sales are cash, enter the proceeds on the form. Ordinarily, some sales will be for cash, some for credit. Your historical records will give you the proportions and a handle on two vital items: How long does it take your average credit customer to pay? How many don't pay at all? Remember: It's not a sale until you get paid.

You can make this section as difficult as you want. However, if most of your credit customers follow 30-day terms, a credit sale in June turns into July cash. If there is a seasonal bias—for instance, if you extend credit to farmers who pay your bills when they sell their crops—then your cash flow must reflect this.

Enter the estimates for cash sales and receivables collections in the appropriate estimate columns. Sales are clearly the most important source of cash inflow. Many of your cost figures depend upon your sales level. If you plan to borrow funds or generate additional equity investments, record the estimated cash inflow amounts in the appropriate months. If you plan to sell any fixed assets, the same procedure should be followed.

> ### Why Budget?
> *"Income of £20.00, expenses of £19.19.6. Result: happiness. Expenses of £20.06. Result: misery."*
> —Charles Dickens
>
> With a budget, you can make sure that your income exceeds your outflow.

You probably have noticed that for cash flow purposes you ignore product list differences. How come? Because your cash flow budget is concerned with cash flow more than with the sources of sales dollars. The subject is plenty complex as it stands.

2. Project Your Monthly Cash Outflows

Once again, as you project monthly outflow, let your P&L projection serve as a guide. Your fixed expenses, already identified, will remain constant every month. Rent, for example, is usually paid monthly. If it is not, spread it in the appropriate manner. Those variable expenses that remain a constant percentage of sales have also been identified; put them down as appropriate. Sales commissions, for example, are tied directly to sales. Your salespeople won't sell if they aren't paid.

Expenses that vary with sales, but not on a constant percentage basis, are the hardest expenses to enter on the form. If the relation is complex, try to find out what it is and adjust the cash flow accordingly. If you aren't sure, be conservative. Greatly increased sales may require increased office staff, which will be reflected as an increase in fixed expenses. This is a step increase, not a smooth curve.

Remember, the "cash-paid-out" items on this form represent cash flowing out of your business, so both dollar amounts and timing are important. Most small businesses need to pay more attention to timing. Often the variations between projections and performance are not a matter of amount, but of time. The cash outflows (and cash inflows) are recorded in the month the disbursement (or payment in cash) is actually made.

This distinction is particularly important when you are planning purchase schedules. By knowing your purchasing, sales, and sales collection cycles, you can often smooth out the peaks and valleys of your cash flow. If, for instance, you run a seasonal gift shop, you may have to incur expenses in June that will be paid in October. Your cash flow should reflect this. Otherwise, you may have a lot of cash floating about and forget that it is already committed to retiring inventory borrowings. It happens.

For some businesses, an entry such as "Reserve for Purchases" is helpful. Plan for a large annual expense or a single payment debt service, and make sure it's budgeted.

All of your disbursements must be recorded on the cash flow/budget projection—all expenses, debt retirement, owner's withdrawals, capital purchases. Cash disbursements that don't get recorded diminish the effectiveness of your budget, so be thorough.

If you plan to expand your business or to acquire or replace equipment, enter those costs and their timing. This affords another chance for review of your plans for the budgetary period. You may find it helpful to apply the same worst/best/most-likely case analysis to your proposed acquisition. Most small companies make major purchases without adequate consideration of alternatives. If you have to disburse cash, make sure it goes into a necessary purchase.

3. Project Operating Data

This is merely a continuation of the process.

First: The monthly cash flow is derived by subtracting the cash outflows from the cash inflows. If the cash flow is negative, it may be temporary and of little concern—but if your projections show a chronic negative cash flow, you have a major problem. You can try to speed up cash flow: increase sales, try for speedier collection of receivables, slow down a bit on payables. But these are not always options.

You may be carrying either too much debt or debt of the wrong kind. If you are using short-term notes to finance acquisition of capital assets or long-term needs, then this will cause major cash flow problems. Ask your banker to review your debt structure with you. Restructuring debt can ease cash flow problems.

Once you are aware of the possible problems that lie ahead, you can do something about them. It's always the unforeseen hazard that causes the biggest problems.

Second: To convert your cash flow budget (which you have now completed) to operating P&L use, add up noncash expenses such as depreciation, and then subtract this from the total. If your company is marginal, this simple test may spotlight areas you can improve.

Review and Revise Quarterly

Review your forecast once again to determine how realistic your projections are. All operating data for the past 12 months should be available. This data helps you keep on track. If you compare your budget with past experience and with industry averages (if available), you can get a measure of how accurate it will be. Large deviations from the past or from averages are warning flags for your use—heed them.

Ask yourself these questions: If you project a dramatic increase in sales, how will those sales be generated? Can you afford those sales? Will you need new people? What are the cash flow implications? Your budget should reflect these concerns clearly—and your notes, as mentioned earlier, should be an aid to rethinking your projections.

The next step in the review process takes time: Test your projections quarterly. This tends to be long enough to smooth out some of the inevitable month-to-month variations, yet short enough to ensure that no problem will be allowed to grow to disastrous proportions.

You may wish to use Rolling Threes: Each month under this review method, you review the current month and the two preceding months, comparing actual with projected figures. This affords a constant and comprehensive review. If substantial differences show up, alter the projections for the next month. Then repeat the process the following month—this tends to smooth out the inevitable month-to-month ripples, while allowing your basic budget to remain pretty much constant.

By checking three-month segments on a monthly basis, you will also find that you gain a heightened awareness of short-term trends, both in your business and the general economy. For instance, personnel turnover tends to make small businesses waver from projections. As the new personnel work into their jobs and become less demanding of the already skilled personnel, the business returns to the projected course.

So review your achievements and budgets on a monthly basis, but don't change your budget unless your review suggests a major error in your projections. A budget is designed to assist in the nominal operations of your business, not in unpredictable variations that are felt for only a week or a month. Of course, you will want to note the impact of these extraordinary events— and perhaps keep a log of them. Sometimes extraordinary events, seen from a longer point of view, form a subtle pattern.

To the cash on hand at the beginning of the period, add cash inflows and subtract cash outflows. The total is your new cash position for the next month. Once more: By comparing your projections to the actual figures, you will get a handle on how well your projections and your budget are working out. If there are extreme variations, check further, although you'll be well advised to check item by item to ensure that your budget is working and being followed.

Shortage or Surplus? Pin It Down

If you have a temporary cash shortage, look for the cause. Ask why that cash shortage is there—your forecast will help. A problem defined is a problem half solved.

The key to effective management is knowing what is going on, what has gone on, and where your business is heading. By planning, you avert problems. By following your budget, you render your cash flow as stable as possible, which in turn makes planning more effective.

Suppose you have a temporary cash surplus. Locate the cause. Maybe you are doing something extremely well that you hadn't planned on—or perhaps outside factors are helping you and this is a nonrecurring happenstance. If you know which, you can plan and adjust accordingly. If you don't learn the cause, then you run the risk of either missing future improvements or making severe mistakes.

Cash surpluses may be generated by forgetting to pay a bill. For instance, you may have a trade payable of $1,000 for inventory that you sold for $2,000, and you forgot to pay the credit. The extra $1,000 cash will have to be tracked down; otherwise it will melt away, leaving you short next month.

Don't Be Worried—Be Warned

More likely, though, a cash surplus reflects the conservative bias of the cash flow/budgeting process, and the surplus can then be utilized to make your business more profitable. In this happy case, retire debt ahead of time. Create a cash reserve. Expand. Do whatever your business plan indicates as the best, most logical step.

Companies run on a cash flow budget are more likely to have surplus cash than companies that are not, because use of a budget mandates careful monitoring of cash outflows.

What if all cash outflows are justified, yet planned cash inflow is inadequate and you suffer a net cash outflow? Then you have no choice. You have to generate additional cash somehow or go under. With a cash flow budget at hand, this problem, while severe, is not insuperable. Since you know how much cash you need and when you need it, you have the beginnings of a financing proposal.

In fact, a well-documented cash flow budget will serve as the heart of your financing proposal if you and your business are already known to your banker. It demonstrates that you know what you're doing and that you take all due precautions. Such careful management appeals to bankers.

Why? The cash flow budgeting process shows that you care enough about the future of your business to establish goals and that you have mapped out a route to achieve those goals. The implied discipline is impressive.

Compare Budgeted vs. Actual Performance

Now what?

You have aimed your business in the right direction. Your budget keeps it on track—and this is where the cash flow/budget form comes in handy.

Always determine the reason for a deviation from your budget. You create your budget under optimal conditions. All the information you have, with time to reflect upon it, improved by review and experience, gives you a sound budget. When you deviate from it, as you will, most likely you will do so under less than ideal conditions—panic, confusion, hustle and bustle, constant interruptions.

Decisions made under stress are seldom as fruitful as those made under conditions more conducive to clear thought. So, when a major deviation is forced upon you, jot it down. Keep a notebook to record your reasons, your response, and whether what you did was right or wrong. This will help when you prepare the next version of your budget, and it will also make you think twice before blowing it up.

Do this faithfully, and it pays off. You'll develop:
• an excellent source of current information,
• an accurate test of the projections you have prepared, and
• a fix on trends, good and bad, affecting your business.

Most important, your budget will reduce the uncertainties inherent in decision making and allow you to make the best decisions for your business.

For instance, your budget can alert you to the need to hire more employees if you need a higher level of output to survive, and it can tell you when to hire them. It can tell you what expansion will do to your cash position, now and in the long run. It can help you pin down timing on major capital expenditures so you won't have to purchase major items before you are ready. You'll be protected against impulsive commitment of funds. By scrutinizing major deals—as your budget compels—you may spot flaws beforehand or new and more exciting applications. Budgeting works for you either way.

Look for Early Trends

In any event, first project your sales, then your expenses for the budgeting period. Then, using the insights and information of your P&L forecast, establish a monthly cash flow, listing your projected cash inflows and outflows in the columns headed "estimate." In the columns headed "actual," record the actual amounts, line by line, on a monthly basis (see page 68). This affords a chance to spot trends and deviations early—so they can be understood, managed, and utilized.

Finally, review and revise your forecast/cash flow budget as necessary. Try to keep your balance on revisions. If you frequently tinker with your budget, it won't help you maintain direction. On the other hand, a budget shouldn't be a straitjacket; if you have sufficient reason to change your budget, change it.

Frederick Adler, a well-known New York venture capitalist, once had T-shirts made up that stated "Happiness Is Positive Cash Flow." Your cash flow budget will result in positive cash flow—and some measure of commercial happiness.

For an action plan, see page 70.

Preparation of Profit-and-Loss Projection *(see right)*

1. Project annual sales

   • Left-hand column: worst possible results (low figures)

   • Right-hand column: best possible results (high figures)

2. Project annual expenses—worst and best conditions

   • Variable expenses

   • Semi-variable expenses

   • Fixed expenses

3. Compare "worst" and "best" projections, prepare reasonable forecast with figures somewhere in between, and review.

Profit-and-Loss Projection

		LOW	MOST LIKELY	HIGH
Sales	Product/Service Line A	$_____	$_____	$_____
	Product/Service Line B	_____	_____	_____
	Product/Service Line C	_____	_____	_____
	Total Sales Revenue	$_____	$_____	$_____
Cost of Goods Sold	Line A	$_____	$_____	$_____
	Line B	_____	_____	_____
	Line C	_____	_____	_____
	Total Cost of Goods Sold	$_____	$_____	$_____
	Gross Profit	$_____	$_____	$_____
Expenses*				
Variable	Payroll	$_____	$_____	$_____
	Sales commissions	_____	_____	_____
	Freight	_____	_____	_____
	Travel and entertainment	_____	_____	_____
	Sales tax	_____	_____	_____
Semi-variable	Advertising and promotion	_____	_____	_____
	FICA/payroll taxes	_____	_____	_____
	Supplies	_____	_____	_____
	Telephone	_____	_____	_____
	Auto and transport	_____	_____	_____
	Postage	_____	_____	_____
	Payroll	_____	_____	_____
	Interest	_____	_____	_____
	Insurance	_____	_____	_____
Fixed	Dues and subscriptions	_____	_____	_____
	Bank charges	_____	_____	_____
	Rent	_____	_____	_____
	Utilities	_____	_____	_____
	Property taxes	_____	_____	_____
	Office expenses	_____	_____	_____
	Total Expenses	$_____	$_____	$_____
	Profit Before Depreciation	$_____	$_____	$_____
	Depreciation	_____	_____	_____
	Net Profit	$_____	$_____	$_____

*The expense items have been arbitrarily assigned to variable, semi-variable, and fixed categories. Expense items for your business may differ. Check with your accountant.

Cash Flow Projection Chart

Year: _____

(Use Whole Dollars)	$	Estimate	%	$	Actual	%
1. Cash on hand (beginning of month)						
2. Cash receipts						
a) Cash sales						
b) Collections from credit accounts						
c) Loan or other cash injection (specify)						
3. Total cash receipts (2a+2b+2c)						
4. Total cash available						
(Before cash out, 1 + 3)						
5. Cash paid out						
Purchases						
Business taxes, licenses						
Employer's share Social Security						
Unemployment						
Rent						
Repairs and maintenance						
Gross salaries						
Insurance						
Professional fees						
Commissions						
Interest and bank charges						
Advertising						
Auto/truck						

Dues and subscriptions			
Office supplies			
Telephone			
Utilities			
Operating supplies			
Travel			
Laundry and uniform			
Entertainment			
Contract services			
Miscellaneous			
Subtotal			
Loan principal payment			
Capital purchases (specify)			
Other start-up costs			
Owner's withdrawal			
6. Total cash paid out			
7. Cash position			
End of month (4 minus 6)			
Essential operating data			
a) Non-cash flow information			
Sales volume (dollars)			
b) Accounts receivable (end of month)			
c) Bad debts (end of month)			
d) Inventory on hand (end of month)			
e) Accounts payable (end of month)			
f) Depreciation			

Forecasting and Cash Flow Budgeting

❑ Set business guidelines and goals.

❑ Review current economic and business conditions; consider how they will affect your business.

❑ Forecast sales for the budget period.

❑ Forecast expenses for the budget period.

❑ Prepare a profit-and-loss projection.

❑ Run a reality check on the numbers. Compare them to your goals, trade figures, and historical figures.

❑ Project monthly cash inflows for the budget period.

❑ Project monthly cash disbursements (outflows) for the budget period.

❑ Project operating data. Move controllable items about to achieve the best positive cash flow possible.

❑ Prepare your cash flow budget: the "finished" cash flow projection. Look for periods of negative cash flow, as well as unusually positive periods.

❑ Compare budgeted with actual performance monthly.

❑ Review performance and recast forecasts (both P&L and cash flow) annually or as needed.

CHAPTER 7

Cash Flow Management

Knowing how to manage your cash flow (and hence financing) can mean the difference between succeeding brilliantly and failing dismally. Cash flow spells survival for every business. Manage cash flow effectively, and your business works. Costs are in order. Sales and collection efforts work together, margins are protected, market share is growing, and all is right with your commercial world.

If your cash flow is not well managed, then sooner or later your business goes under. It's that simple. A positive cash flow is one where cash comes in faster than it goes out. Maintain this—which includes paying your bills on time as well as making investments in growth—and a lot of other business problems melt. If you need more capital or more debt to grow, you can get it on reasonable terms. You can try out new ideas, products, markets.

The corollary is that if cash flow is mismanaged, you can't do much more than struggle to stay afloat.

Most businesses are somewhere in between these two poles. They have a positive cash flow and meet their bills, earn a modest profit, and can afford to seek new business. But sometimes—more often than they like—they find themselves suffering from a negative cash flow. On balance, they should end up in the black—but there can be some grim times in the middle.

The nut, which is comprised of monthly fixed expenses that must be paid on a regular basis—that is, their schedules can't be tampered with—is the silent strangler of cash flow.

What causes cash flow blues? There are three major causes: The nut gets imperceptibly bigger, a few costs slip out of control, or some sales don't turn into cash on time. There are others, but these are the big ones. This chapter outlines the steps to take to improve a less-than-optimal cash flow performance. The steps aren't magical or mysterious, but they work. Some of them are painful. Cutting the nut can be difficult. Giving up a future profit (perhaps illusory) to preserve the business can be painful. When you're singing the cash flow blues, the present may seem grim, but expectations for the future may seem pretty alluring.

Most of the steps look simpler than they are. Stick with them. Cash flow problems are caused by the slow accretion of small expenditures over a long period of time.

Manage for Survival First

The first aim of any business is to remain in business. All decisions should be made with this in mind.

Cash flow difficulties kill more small businesses than any other cause. This is partly due to the thin capitalization such businesses ordinarily have, but is also due to the subtle, insidious nature of cash flow problems.

Cash flow problems sneak up on you. A major calamity—such as the failure of a major supplier, which in turn causes the loss of several month's sales—is the exception. More often, cash flow trouble is the aggregate result of many tiny errors.

Consider the case of the company that, in anticipation of a major new piece of business, hired extra people, moved to a larger, more expensive location, took on some new equipment, spent a lot of selling time in negotiations with the other parties to the contract, and ended up in a cash bind. To solve the cash bind, it took on new short-term debt—and then the first payment under the contract was put off for six months.

The result? The company joined the legion singing the cash flow blues.

All of the moves it made were—up to a point—sensible. When any business embarks on a period of sharp growth, some cash flow lag is inevitable. More fixed assets will be needed. New personnel (with the implied training costs) will be needed. More working capital is required to float the higher levels of inventory and receivables.

But it all hinges on getting paid—what amounts, and when.

What can be done to avoid a similar cash crunch in the future? Keep the business's survival in mind first. By first securing the contract—and making sure of the payment schedule—you improve cash flow and ensure that the business survives even if negotiations hit a snag.

The best cash flow management policy is based on keeping the business solvent—that is, always able to meet current obligations. Though most businesspeople agree with that policy in principle, temptations to expand or gear up for a certain piece of business can sabotage cash flow. Most simply put, expenditures you don't incur won't hurt your cash flow.

Five Severe Warning Signs of Cash Flow Problems

1. Decreased liquidity: running out of working capital.
2. Overtrading: turning inventories faster than trade averages.
3. Excessive short-term debt.
4. Missing discounts: payables over terms.
5. Slow collections: outstanding receivables piling up.

List Cash Inflows

There are only four sources of cash:
1. Operating profits
2. Sale of fixed assets
3. New investment
4. New debt

Of the four, operating profits are by far the most important. The other three sources are at best sporadic. At times, the sale (and sometimes the lease-back) of fixed assets is the best source of cash. New investment from you may be the only way to keep your business going. At times new debt makes the most sense.

In the long run, if your business doesn't take in more cash than it must lay out, you won't have a business. Occasionally, we all lose sight of the importance of operating profitability. If you don't produce operating profits, or can't show where they will come from soon, then no one in his or her right mind would invest in your business or lend money to you. That's because if a business doesn't make a cash flow profit on operations, it goes under.

Managing for cash flow is managing for survival. To manage your cash flow, start by looking at your past performance. Unless you have good reasons to expect differently, your business will repeat the same general patterns year after year. For example, one business is tied to a limited number of large customers. While the number of customers is growing, the company's basic profile remains the same. This company confidently expects to do more than 80% of its dollar sales volume between October and March, with much of the cash coming in January, due to the budget cycles of its largest customers. It doesn't anticipate any changes in this pattern and has taken the cash flow implications into its planning efforts.

Your business has a definite cash flow cycle. Look for it. Start by listing the cash inflows on a calendar (or on index cards), paying particular attention to when the cash comes in. Creating a receivable is one thing—getting the cash in is another, and it's more important for most businesses. A huge uncollected receivable is a major source of the cash flow blues. Customers who pay late or slowly create cash shortages. Even these can be planned for by analyzing the effect of different collection periods on cash flow.

You may wish to separate the inflows into four basic categories: Operating Profits, Sale of Fixed Assets, New Investment, and New Debt. Unless your business is based on unusual financing, make sure that you treat the last three as onetime events.

An exception: Seasonal borrowing is such a part of most retailers' plans that there will be little alteration in the amount and timing of the cash inflow from that kind of borrowing from one year to the next. Use your judgment: If you have this debt pattern, include it in your plans.

That leaves operating profits. You have to start with this—every variable expense (expense tied to sales volume) depends on it.

On a month-by-month basis, set down what you expect to receive in actual cash next year. This requires that you know when your customers pay their bills. If you extend credit, you should know from experience. If you are new to the game, ask more experienced players like your banker.

To be conservative, factor in the possibility of late customer payments, even if they have been paying on time. Expect their performance to slide. Many companies look for about 15 to 30 days beyond terms.

If you get a few large orders out of the blue now and again, do not try to count on them to balance your cash flow. It's better by far to be pleasantly surprised. The cost of not getting an order because you weren't prepared for it is far lower than being well prepared for an order that never arrives.

List Cash Outflows

You have unlimited numbers of ways to dribble away cash: payroll, inventory, travel, supplies, advertising, space costs, taxes, and so on.

Start by reviewing last year's budget against last year's disbursement performance. If you don't have a budget, consider whether you need one. A cash flow budget is an essential cost control tool, and not controlling costs is risky.

Look to your budget. The expenses may be constant, but the cash disbursements won't be. For example, suppose your insurance costs $1,200 per year. For an accrual budget, that works out to be $100 per month. (The expense is incurred in equal amounts.) On a cash flow budget, however, the cost might be $100 per month, or $1,200 in March, or $300 a quarter, if that's the payment schedule.

Timing is as important as the dollar amount when you consider cash flow.

Monthly Cash Flow Analysis
June

INFLOWS		OUTFLOWS	
		Disbursements:	
Source	**Amount**	**Fixed**	**Amount**
Customer A	$4800	Rent	$ 275
Customer B	1250	Loan payment	1200
		Variable	
		Printer	$675
		Sales commission	480
Total: $_____		Total: $_____	

Determine when payment has to be made in cash. You want to keep track of when the obligation is incurred, but what matters here is the actual cash disbursement. You might be more comfortable with a $1,200 payment in March than a $300 payment in August; it is a function of *your* cash flow.

For most businesses, cash journals and checkbooks provide the specific historical information on just when you paid bills. If you have been managing for cash flow, this is an easy step. If you have not, it becomes a bit more tricky. The disbursements were probably made sporadically, their timing more dependent on when you had cash available than on when it would be best (from a cash flow standpoint) to pay the bills.

Now list—on the same calendars or other sheets you used for the prospective inflows—when you expect to be making specific cash disbursements. These will fall into two main groups: fixed and variable.

Fixed monthly disbursements (such as office and administrative payroll, insurance, utilities and basic telephone, interest on principal payments on term loans, rent, or mortgage) present a special problem.

A normal increase in the nut is understandable if not inevitable. The cost of everything rises because inflation pushes it up. Salaries go up; otherwise you lose your best people. The cost of supplies goes up. Maintenance and utility costs go up.

Your task is to monitor and resist increases in fixed costs. Those single costs may appear innocuous, but on a yearly basis, they add up.

Kept low, your nut represents the necessary costs of doing business. Not checked against a budget, it will choke your business—like many people, you'll be left wondering why that large increase in sales never got to the bottom line. And why you suddenly ran out of cash. The response to this kind of problem is frequently to borrow a little more for working capital on a term basis. This merely drives the nut up further, compounding the problem and making it even more difficult to earn an operating profit.

Variable costs are tricky also. If you face a period of sharp growth, the costs specifically associated with that growth tend to shoot up faster than receipts turn to cash, and the result is strangulation of the cash flow. To prevent this, you will probably need financing; it is extremely unusual to be able to finance fast growth out of your operating profits.

If you expect continued sharp growth, make your projections accordingly. If you do anticipate a major shift in how you do business, then seek help from your accountant.

Look for Cash Flow Trends

Much of the difficulty of management lies in details. In the heat of day-to-day operations, you can lose sight of important trends. If you practice deviation analysis, a formal method of comparing actual against budgeted performance on a monthly and a year-to-date basis, you won't miss many cash flow danger signals.

At the very least, you should sit down monthly and try to discern whether cash income is on target with projections and whether the nut is being held in check. Major cash outlays usually get accorded a lot of thought; minor ones do not, and businesses suffer as a result.

If cash inflow lags behind outflow, you have a problem, one you should address immediately. On the other hand, if cash inflow is ahead of outflow, then you may have the happy discovery of idle cash—money you can put to another use, such as fueling growth, retiring debt and lowering the nut, trying out a new market, or making a new product.

On a large calendar, match up (by week or by month) cash inflows and outflows. Many successful businesses do this on a daily basis with the help of spreadsheets and software.

Sum up both inflows and outflows. Are they changing? Keep year-to-date as well as monthly records to smooth out temporary aberrations and spotlight really subtle trends that develop over a period of months.

Example: If cash disbursements are being made later and later each month, or if a major customer cancels a large order that you had slotted to provide 85% of June's cash flow. (Incidentally, concentrating your business in a few accounts may be risky. For survival, you do better to have 100 customers paying $1,000 apiece than one who pays $100,000—the chances are slight that you would lose 100 customers at one time.)

But the obvious dramas rarely put a business in a hopeless position. The really dangerous problem is the one you don't see until it's almost too late—a characteristic of cash flow problems.

Cash and the Calendar

An alert cash flow manager keeps an eye not on cash receipts or on cash demands as average quantities, but on cash as a function of the calendar.

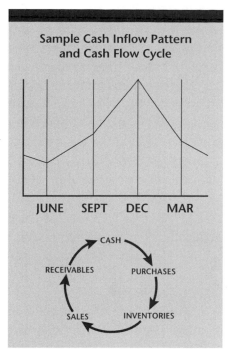

Sample Cash Inflow Pattern and Cash Flow Cycle

On an income statement, uncollected receivables are considered revenues and are a component of measuring a company's performance from one reporting period to another. But in cash flow analysis, receivables are worthless until they turn into real money. Accounts receivable turnover determines *when* you'll have cash to meet payables and other obligations. Because cash flow analysis tracks cash over periods of time—essentially, when cash in must go back out—the projection of how many days it takes for your business to convert receivables to cash is a significant number.

Here's the basic calculation: Divide your annual sales by 365 to get one day's sales; then divide the amount of your receivables by one day's sales to get the number of days it takes your customers to pay you. For example, $1.2 million in annual sales divided by 365 days equals $3,288; $172,000 in receivables divided by $3,288 equals 52.3 days. If, by similar calculation, you're paying your suppliers in 60 days, you're getting 7.7 days'—more than a week's—free use of their money.

Dollar amount (either coming in or going out) per time period is the crucial cash flow consideration. A spreadsheet can trace the stage-by-stage impact of proposed business decisions on the company's cash account, enabling management to compare when a certain amount of cash is needed with projections of when that cash would come back out as revenues.

Leverage

Here's cash flow's fundamental leverage rule: Get your customers to pay you as soon as possible (preferably in advance). Get your vendors to let you take your sweet time paying *them* (preferably within 60 to 90 days).

The premise is that every dollar collected in receivables this morning that isn't needed for payables until tonight is yours to multiply all day. A business might take advantage of that otherwise fallow interval by buying raw material with the dollar at 9 a.m., manufacturing something out of that material, and selling the finished item for $2 at 10 a.m.; buying twice as much material with the $2 it now has and selling two items for $4 at 11 a.m.; buying four times as much material for $4 and selling four items for $8 at noon, and so on. At that rate, by 5 p.m., when the dollar must be dispatched to its now-rightful owner, the company has 255 more dollars than it had at 9 a.m. Subtract labor and variable costs, and you're still way ahead.

Spend Now?

It's the nature of small businesses to favor cost saving over cost making, but don't assume that *not* spending cash is the equivalent of protecting cash. Judicious spending can enhance cash flow, returning yet more cash in the timely fashion that positive cash flow calls for. If, instead of draining the cash account by $10,000, you spend a concrete $2,000 on hiring a temporary office worker to dispatch invoices promptly, wouldn't there be an *actual* gain of $8,000 in the year's ending cash balance? That's one illustration of how spending now can have positive future effects on cash flow.

Control Cash Outflows

When a cash flow problem rears its head, the natural urge is to try to build up sales and pare expenses. That's fine, but all too often the wrong costs are cut and the least likely customers pursued. Your quickest return will usually come from cutting the nut.

How? By rescheduling payments, you can almost always gain several weeks grace without losing the respect of your suppliers and creditors. Your banker, for example, would much prefer that you ask to make interest-only payments to ease you through a cash crunch than have you skip payments without any explanation at all. If you took your banker's advice in good times (when the loan was made) you should take it in bad times as well. Take it now, from an expert, when the cash flow is tight.

You can't tamper with fixed payments that are legally tied to a schedule. You cannot shift paydays about on whim, but other payments are often movable, and to your benefit. Make a list of "must" and "hold" payments.

To "lean on trade" (stall payment without explanation until your creditors put lighted matches under your feet) is often recommended by the irresponsible. This is an utterly foolish way to deal with a cash flow problem, and you can only make enemies.

If you cannot make a payment on time, don't compound the problem. Your creditors know when you miss a payment. To say, "The check is in the mail" or to send an empty envelope or an unsigned check, or to pull any of thousands of other stunts won't help you either. They will make your creditors angry, and angry creditors will either pull the plug or put you on a cash-only basis.

Call your creditors. Explain the problem. Explain how you plan to handle it and perhaps offer to make partial payments until things turn around. You will probably be given a chance to breathe.

Put yourself in their shoes: If one of your customers asked for a reduced payment plan because of a cash crunch, while another refused to return your calls and letters, which one would you carry?

Another possible source of relief is to refinance debt. It takes longer than rescheduling monthly payments and may be either expensive or impossible. However, if you have a monthly debt payment of $1,000, it may be better to refinance at $700 a month, even if the interest rate is substantially higher. Your nut will be lower, which will ease a major cash flow crisis. As your cash position improves, you might then be able to reduce the principal—but that's another kind of cash flow device.

Rescheduling works. Refinancing works. And reducing the nut always helps in a cash flow crisis. Your aim throughout is to match up inflows and outflows, with the outflows always following the inflows. If you can arrange to do this without cutting yourself off from the possibility of growing (ultra-conservatism doesn't pay a big dividend in growth), you won't be sorry.

Summary

If you manage your business for cash flow, you accomplish several benefits:

1. You will have your attention firmly riveted on generating and maintaining operating profits.
2. You will be compelled to work within the bounds of a budget geared to your own cash flow needs; this prevents careless errors that cut profitability.
3. You will find that you can grow—and secure the necessary financing to do so with minimal risk.

Cash Flow Management

❏ Manage for survival. You can't make a profit if you aren't in business.

❏ List cash inflows from all sources, by amount and date. Summarize to keep it manageable.

❏ Study and understand your cash flow cycle.

❏ List cash outflows. What patterns do they display? Which can be juggled to ease cash flow squeezes?

❏ Look for long-term cash flow trends.

❏ Control cash outflows by using your cash flow budget. Check performance monthly against budget.

CHAPTER 8

Managing Positive Cash Flow

Most cash flow problems are a result of negative cash flow—a slow attrition of the company's ability to meet current bills, panic over eroding sales, bankruptcy, or dissolution of the business if the flow isn't reversed.

But positive cash flow, desirable though it is, brings problems of its own. Properly managed, positive cash flow allows you to increase profits, gain greater market share, invest in other businesses, pay your employees and yourself dividends, and please your bankers and investors.

Managed imprudently, positive cash flow can torpedo your business. Approach an extended period of positive cash flow the same way you'd approach any other business opportunity: with caution.

Determine the Source of the Positive Cash Flow

Positive cash flow—the increase in cash in your business over a period of time—can come from a number of sources. Not all of them are due to good management. You could experience improved cash flow while going broke. Here are a few examples:

- Stop paying your bills. While this might look good from a cash flow viewpoint, it will put you out of business.
- Forget to pay taxes. More than one company has done this, but borrow-

ing from Uncle Sam is expensive.

- A credulous investor may have popped a substantial sum of cash into your failing enterprise.

Not all sources of positive cash flow are either beneficial or long-lasting. The source of positive cash flow can be neutral:

- You have just landed a major contract, and the retainer is paid in advance.
- Your business is seasonal, and this is the time of year when the money is rolling in.
- Stymied by lack of capital, you have just acquired a new partner or sold some equity in your business.
- You accrue funds all year to make a lump-sum payment into a pension plan, and the bill is due next month.

Most of the time, positive cash flow comes from a combination of these neutral (and benign, if recognized) sources, with some operating cash flow tossed in. The best sources of positive cash flow—and the ones all businesses strive for—are these:

- You are really making a lot of money.
- Sales are up, costs are down.
- Prior investments pay off.

Basically, positive cash flow comes from a very limited number of sources: new capital, new debt, sale of assets, and operations. The first three are limited, because if the fourth doesn't chip in regularly, you run out of investors, your creditors pull the plug, and there are no assets to sell.

Hence the need to determine the sources of positive cash flow in your company. Once you have identified them, your strategies for using the excess cash can be formulated—but not before. For example, you might choose an aggressive strategy if the sources include a new contract, some operating efficiencies due to investment in new equipment, and a few deferred expenses. However, if the sources are deferred expenses, unpaid taxes, and sale of your one money-making division, quite another strategy is called for.

Project Future Cash Flow

If you don't have a cash flow projection to guide your business, you run greater risks than you should. A cash flow budget helps you in many ways.

1. *You can identify all sources of cash inflow, on a month-to-month basis.* If you receive progress payments, when are they due? If your business is seasonal, when do you get cash? If you have a lot of receivables, when do they come due?

Since there are only four sources of cash (new debt, new investment, sale of assets, and operations), you can estimate cash inflows. List the sources of cash, breaking operating sources into Accounts Receivable, Cash Sales, and Sale of Cash Instruments. Show weekly or biweekly, for a one-month period, what cash inflow you anticipate. See below for an example.

2. *You can identify the uses of cash on the same schedule.* Don't aim for accounting perfection here. It's better to use rounded figures and get a rough idea than it is to bog down in precise figures. Uses of cash are limited also: accounts payable, cash expenses, debt service, payroll, and other (for loose ends). Your bookkeeper should be able to provide these figures.

A Simple Cash Flow Projection

Cash on hand: $1,250

LINE ITEM	WEEKLY	BIWEEKLY	MONTHLY
Sources			
Operations			
Accounts Rec.	$300.00	0.00	$4750.00
Cash Sales	750.00	0.00	0.00
Sale of Cash Inst.	0.00	0.00	0.00
New Debt			
New Investment			
Sale of Assets			
Uses			
Accounts Payable	$ 0.00	$600.00	$500.00
Cash Expenses	125.00	0.00	0.00
Debt Service	0.00	0.00	0.00
Payroll	0.00	1375.00	400.00
Other	200.00	200.00	200.00
Net Period Flow			
Weekly	$725.00		
Biweekly		($1450.00)	
Monthly			$600.00

The table above indicates a typical problem with cash flow management. While there is an occasional week of substantial positive cash flow, there is also at least one week of substantial negative cash flow offsetting it. The usual strategy here would be to apply only monthly net cash flows to nonoperational items. Intermonth surplus—if any—would then be placed in a money market account or similar cash instrument.

3. *List major anticipated expenditures and inflows for one year.* For example, if one of your customers prepays in January for the year, while one of your suppliers has to be prepaid in March for a six-month supply of raw material, you must take these cash flow oddities into account. Your aim: as few surprises as possible. Your goal is to be able to accrue cash (or credit on a line of credit) to meet operating obligations as they fall due.

4. *Subtract outflows from inflows on the same schedule as in steps 1 and 2.*

Once you have the next month projected, apply the same steps to the next quarter and the next year. While you may have this information available now, it should be updated as your business circumstances change. If you do get an increase in business, it will result in a major cost increase to service the sales.

Once you have a grasp of the cash flow picture for the next several months, you will understand your cash needs too. You may find, for example, that some of the idle cash can be salted away for future growth, while some will have to be available to meet next month's cash shortfall.

Establish Priorities for Your Cash Flow

Positive cash flow from operations creates opportunities to make more money. The way to use your cash flow will best be chosen by looking at the rate of return for each available option. Those items with the greatest potential impact on your bottom line are those that either increase revenue (without driving up fixed costs too fast) or decrease expenses (new equipment, for example).

Suppose your balance sheet looks like the one on page 86. Reducing short-term debt of $18,500 on a line of credit would be a priority. So would increasing inventories and advertising. The question becomes: Which option makes the most sense?

You will note that the number-one

Sales and Expenses

Increased sales and increased expenses go together. But not in a smooth line, particularly for growing businesses. If you anticipate a substantial increase in sales over the next year, ask your accountant what this will mean in terms of:

- Operating margins

- Fixed costs (New plant and equipment? Increased overhead and administrative costs?)

- Profitability

Ask yourself what it will mean in terms of managerial ability and time.

Expenses (both in dollars and in management time) tend to rise in steps, not smoothly with sales. A modest increase in sales may result in greatly increased profits, because fixed expenses won't be increased. But a major sales increase can actually result in lowered profitability—and negative cash flow—if fixed expenses take an upward leap.

priority is reduction of short-term debt. Although the first two items (salaries and taxes, payables) will probably have a more dramatic effect on the company than debt reduction, keep in mind that it is easier to deposit cash against a line of credit than it is to spend it wisely. Any money not needed for immediate requirements should be used to pay down a line of credit for two significant reasons:

1. You will save substantial interest costs.

2. As a rule of thumb, your banker will be more amenable to increasing your credit line when it's necessary if he or she can see periods when your line was only partially extended.

Research Investment Strategies and Opportunities

There are all too many ways to invest excess cash. Some of the questions to ask yourself—once the immediate priorities have been satisfied—include:

1. *Security.* How safe is your money, and will it be there when you need it?

2. *Liquidity.* While a long-term, high-rate certificate of deposit has its uses, what happens if you need the money next month, not two years from now?

3. *Yield.* Before investing, would the money earn more if reinvested in your company than if it were put into a cash management account? Or would a short-term investment provide the right balance of yield and liquidity for your company?

4. *Time required.* If your bank has a money market account, it might make more sense to use it than to seek out the best yield yourself.

Check around. If you enjoy substantial positive cash flow and want to make your cash work for you, start by asking your banker. This serves several purposes. Compensating balances may help lower your credit costs, allow you increased borrowing capacity should a need arise, and make you a more desirable bank customer.

Keep your aims clear, however. You want safety and liquidity first, then yield. This doesn't mean to let excess cash idle, just that your business should make its profits on operations, not on investments.

Choose the Appropriate Strategy and Stick to It

Based on your analysis of your business's needs and opportunities, you can now begin to maximize the return on your excess cash. Be consistent, and be sure that your strategies are part of the long-term business plan.

For example, suppose that you have asked your bank to set up a sweep account to be used whenever balances rise above a preset limit. This allows current obligations to be funded, yet makes sure that idle funds will do some

Balance Sheet:
Your Company
December 31, 1999

Current Assets:

Cash	$1,250
Accounts Rec.	6,725
Deposits	1,420
Inventory	18,300
Subtotal:	$27,695

Fixed Assets:

Furniture & Equipment	$3,100
Capitalized Leases	5,695
Start-up Costs	1,780
Less Accum. Deprec.	(4,310)
Subtotal:	$6,265
TOTAL ASSETS:	$33,960

Current Liabilities:

Trade Payables	$1,830
Accrued Salaries & Taxes	2,700
Current Por. Cap. Leases	1,300
Demand Note Payable	18,500
Subtotal:	$24,330

Long-Term Debt

Capitalized Lease Oblig.	$2,295
Subtotal:	$2,295

Owner's Equity

100 Shares Common Stock	$1,000
Paid in Capital	19,000
Retained Earnings (Loss)	(15,765)
Fiscal Year Net Profit	3,100
Subtotal:	$7,335

Total Liabilities & Equity:	**$33,960**

work for you. The excess cash will be swept daily into a high-interest money market account, immediately available if needed for operational purposes.

By keeping borrowing low, you reduce interest costs. In most cases, interest you pay is higher than interest you would receive from an investment. On the other hand, there can be good reasons to keep cash liquid rather than paying down a line of credit or reducing other debt.

For example, you may be approaching year-end, and you want to be able to use your financial statements for raising more debt or new equity investment. A strong acid test ratio (cash and near cash divided by current liabilities) can make investors drool—and with a positive cash flow, handling long-term debt would not be a problem. "Prettying up" your balance sheet can pay off, whether you are a multinational company, a corner store, or somewhere in between.

The important thing is that you adapt your cash flow strategy to your business plan. If you know what cash you will need, when you will need it, and why, you can make consistently fine decisions.

Once you adopt a strategy, stick to it until conditions change. Note the qualifier: *until conditions change.* No strategy is good forever, and no strategy works if it isn't implemented.

The priority list refers to your business plan, your cash budget, and the credit line limit of $30,000. Your notes can spell the difference between dreaming and achievement.

Description	Amount	Notes
1. Reduce credit line	$_____	_____
	_____	_____
	_____	_____
	_____	_____
2. Increase inventory	$_____	_____
	_____	_____
	_____	_____
	_____	_____
3. Increase advertising	$_____	_____
	_____	_____
	_____	_____
	_____	_____

Action Plan

Managing Positive Cash Flow

❏ Determine the source of the positive cash flow. Is it from operations? Or from less desirable sources?

❏ Project future cash flow: weekly, monthly, yearly (see format on page 83).

❏ Create a short-term and long-range cash plan. The cash flow plan/budget represents a projection of all cash receipts and disbursements. These include both near-term working capital cash flows and longer-range capital expenditures and receipts. A cash flow budget (see Chapter 6) is the single financial tool that can tie together all parts of a strategic five-year plan. It blends near-term (one to three months) cash needs, the one-year P&L cash budget for short-term operating cash management, and the long-range (five years) capital budget.

A good cash flow budget, properly prepared and closely monitored on a weekly basis, will enable you to come to terms with cash flow. The process provides at least eight advantages to accelerate growth:

1. Cash flow peaks and valleys can be anticipated.
2. Borrowing costs can be reduced, flowing straight through to profit and cash dividends.
3. Financing through loans and/or new equity can be better planned and more favorable terms obtained.
4. Cash flow discounts can be taken.
5. Purchasing costs can be reduced by more economical quantity purchases.
6. Cash flow from collections can be speeded up, and payables can be stretched out.
7. Spare cash can be invested more timely, at higher return rates.
8. Cost controls can be tightened to cut overhead.

❑ Establish priorities for investing excess cash flow. Check it against your business plan.

❑ Research investment strategies and opportunities. Choose the appropriate strategy and stick to it.

CHAPTER 9

Financial Controls

In most small and growing companies, the two most important financial controls regulate costs and liquidity. These are the cash flow budget and the projected income statement. Use of these controls presupposes that you have adequate record-keeping and accounting systems. Most small-business software provide charts of accounts and numerous reporting features, so, assuming your data is entered accurately, you should be able to easily generate:

1. monthly income statements,
2. quarterly cash flow projections,
3. annual income statement and balance sheet,
4. projections—income statement, balance sheet, and cash flow, and
5. budgets for operations and capital expenditures.

In a stable business, sales are largely predictable. Budgets can be based on extrapolations from prior years' experience. But for a growing business, the problems are more complex.

First, growing companies commonly face severe cash flow problems. As sales go up, so do receivables. While your business may be showing excellent profits, you may find that your bank balance has vanished: You're in the midst of a liquidity crisis. Higher sales levels tend to drive fixed costs up in dispropor-tionate steps. Often the company cannot afford to undertake new sales without acquiring new debt (expensive) or selling equity in the business (unpalatable).

Second, if a company grows rapidly, it overworks its capital. Consequently, its financial ratios (which are indicators to bankers and other financing sources) fail to meet criteria for new debt. This can happen even while your company is growing rapidly in value. Unfortunately, financing sources tend to be wary of that combination of distorted cash flow and depleted working capital caused by growth.

Is there a solution?

Yes—at least a partial one. To soften the cash flow and capital problems, you have to look ahead. Try to prepare for the crunch before it comes, and trim costs accordingly.

One way to accomplish this is to use variance reports. A variance report displays variations in performance from previously established performance guidelines. These are usually drawn from cash flow budgets and income statement projections.

Variance reports, prepared regularly (usually monthly or weekly):

• *Compel attention to budgets without excessive attention to detail.* Budgets are often ignored because of the detail involved. The variance report system minimizes detail and maximizes useful information. You are able to detect serious variations. Then, and only then, is it necessary to draw on detailed information.

• *Help focus your attention on real problems.* Most of us use our time inefficiently. One of the best uses of your time is solving problems that affect the business before they get out of hand. If the variance report shows a cost slipping out of control or a new efficiency in production, you know where to direct your efforts.

• *Provide the basis for evaluating performance.* Variance reports are highly effective teaching tools. A department that consistently achieves or exceeds the standards implicit in these reports merits attention. What is being done well?

• *Help you and your financial advisers look ahead to avert cash flow and capital problems.* One of the most common problems for a growing company is that as sales and output go up, costs slide out of control. This may be due to a number of subtle causes, but most of the time, it's because basic cost information is ignored. Variance reports allow you to set cost guidelines and follow major costs.

Your application of variance reports will be unique. Be sure to get competent professional help establishing standards and guidelines if you think you need it. In most businesses that have never used a variance report system, the cost of professional help and implementation will immediately be offset by the savings.

Management at Koehler Mfg. experienced a rude awakening—its best-selling product line, lead acid batteries, was devouring company profits. The Marlborough, Mass., company had dutifully accounted for the costs of processing and disposing of the hazardous by-products of battery manufacturing. Even with those expenses, the books showed that the batteries were emphatically profitable. The books, however, were wrong.

Koehler's confusion is far from unique. It's quite possible that your most profitable product is actually a loser and that your best customers are costing you much more than they're worth. Does your company sell more than a dozen or so products? Are annual sales more than $3 million? Are your customers' buying patterns wildly divergent? If so, you may not know your costs as well as you think you do.

Until Koehler installed NetProphet (Sapling Corp., 888-335-5051), an activity-based cost-accounting package, nobody knew that certain administrative costs were attributable to the battery business. When that information emerged, the product's profitability dropped by nearly 30%. The company hadn't considered product-specific expenses incurred while it was dealing with environmental officials, applying for permits, and filing compliance reports.

Acquire Cost Data

Cost accounting is primarily a function of the manufacturing process. It is something that accountants learn in-depth, so they are the best source for setting up a system that will generate the data you need. Software is also available to help with activity-based costing (ABC). Here are the numbers you will need to crunch to acquire good cost data:

1. How long the operation takes and how that time is distributed (work flow analysis helps here)
2. What the time costs—including idle time, pauses, and interruptions
3. What materials costs are involved
4. What administrative overhead costs are for the operation

If you attempt to design a system to identify these costs, you'll drown in detail. Pay your accountant to do it.

Put realistic time and dollar costs on each product or service. As you and your accountant plow through the cost data and discuss operations with your employees (who will usually have good ideas on how to improve work flow), you will begin to spot opportunities for immediate savings. This is an instant bonus—but the real savings will show up later, when budgets based on actual times and costs are implemented.

Suppose you have four different product lines. Do you know which ones are profitable? Which are less profitable? Which are predictable and which are not? Your accountant should be able to provide this level of information.

Unless you know how much a product or service costs and why it costs that much, you can't control costs (and benefit from the learning curve as you begin to understand the process more deeply) and you can't price your product or service effectively. More than one company has energetically expanded sales of items they were losing money on, thinking that the losses will turn to profits after enough volume is reached. It doesn't work that way.

Case: The New ABC

"We're basically your typical widget shop," says Hugh Pinkus, vice-president of finance for Transparent Container, a $21-million manufacturer of plastic containers. But two years ago, the Berkeley, Ill., company made an atypical decision that "helped us keep boosting our revenues and profit margins during the last recession," says Pinkus. Transparent adopted an accounting method known as activity-based costing (ABC), which helps managers identify all activities involved in their production processes and thus isolate costs.

This method allowed Pinkus to recognize that "we were failing to consider all kinds of corporate expenses in our pricing model. For example, the more our receiving dock is used on an order, the more expensive that order becomes to fulfill. Those kinds of costs had slipped past our "attention."

At many growing companies, managers quickly lose sight of the complex string of production costs and related activities. "In the past, if one job required twice as much machine time as another, we'd probably just price it twice as high—and we might have lost that job," says Pinkus. "Now we realize that such a job really just consumes more electricity and is not really much more expensive. Another job, requiring more customer service or multiple shipments, might be worth the higher price tag instead."

Prepare Monthly Income Statement and Cash Flow Projections

These projections allow you to establish useful budgets. Why do you need both? To help you achieve the aims of any budget: preservation of liquidity and advantageous use of available capital.

Your income statement projections contain, in condensed form, sales and expense information. Since these intimately affect your balance sheet (in the long run, profits from operations are the only way to make the business grow), you need income statements to show how long-term debt will be repaid. These projections are also important if you're going to need capital investments, whether the capital is yours or someone else's.

In the shorter term, the income statement helps avert cash flow and liquidity problems by flagging sales lags (or increases) and expense variances. Used monthly, your variance reports:

1. display the information in your projections,
2. let you know whether your projections are being met, and
3. help you predict cash flow difficulties before they hit.

A sales problem in March can surface as a cash problem in June. If you are aware of the problem by early April, you have ample time to explain to your banker why you'll need short-term funds.

The cash flow projection, on the other hand, is almost exclusively attuned to short-term needs. These projections become your budget. They will become more accurate with experience and good cost data. Cash flow projections are the single most important financial control for most small and growing businesses, but they need to be supported by income statements if the business is to become stable and profitable. It's important to use both.

Prepare Variance Reports

The variance report can be taken directly from the income statement and cash flow projections. Any variance can be tracked to its source with a minimum of effort. If you think you need more detail, then the process is the same.

What you exclude may be as important as what you include, since an exhaustive variance report that tracks down individual paper clips is sure to be ignored, while a report that does not account for labor costs will be useless. Fine-tune to achieve the right level of detail for your reporting purposes.

What are the important variables to keep on top of?

What items can be combined or ignored? If you were limited to 10 pieces of information about operations, what would they be? Too much information is as bad as too little. Then ask: What standards (expressed in dollars) do I need to keep track of these activities?

Your standard costs may be listed by unit or batch, if your business is manufacturing. If your business is a retail or service operation, standard costs will be listed by activity.

Here are some typical sources of variances:

• *Material purchase price variance.* Anything from a raw materials price increase to an alternative vendor will create an unfavorable variance. A favorable variance might occur if a contract price is renegotiated downward, or if an increase in buying volume results in a quantity discount.

• *Labor rate variance.* Although uncommon, a labor rate variance would occur when different workers do the same job, or when wage rates change before being calculated into standard cost.

• *Overhead variance.* Changes in overhead costs can affect a standard unit or activity cost. Such a variance might be the result of a change in lease or maintenance costs.

• *Sales collection variance.* When collection problems consistently affect cash flow, it's wise to measure a sales collection variance.

Variance Report

Month of_____, Year____

	Projected	Actual	Variance
Net Sales	$_____	$_____	$_____
Cash Receipts	_____	_____	_____
Cash Disbursements	_____	_____	_____
Cash Surplus or Deficit	_____	_____	_____
Cash Balance — Month End	_____	_____	_____
Short-Term Debt Required	_____	_____	_____

Comments/Proposed Action _____

_____

_____

_____

_____

Signature _____

Date _____

Track Key Financial and Operating Ratios

The trends of your ratios can be a profitable study. Your monthly financial statements should allow you to calculate all of the ratios on page 89. If you then examine them as they change over a period of three months and discuss them with your banker, you should be able to spot coming liquidity and capital problems.

Three key ratios to follow are current ratio, debt-to-worth, and pretax profit/sales. The current ratio measures ability to meet short-term debts. The debt-to-worth ratio measures ability to assume more long-term debt. Pretax profit/sales ratio measures ability to retire long-term debt.

Your banker will almost certainly wish to follow these ratios over a period of months—the concerns are similar to yours: Can you handle the debt? Are you managing your company efficiently? This would be indicated in part by improving ratios.

Decide what you would like the ratios to be from your forecasts and pro formas. Then check monthly to see how you are doing—is there a significant deviation? If so, is it good or bad? This is another way to apply deviation analysis to your business's performance.

Variance Report

Month of_____, Year____

	Projected	Actual	Variance
Product A	_____	_____	_____
Product B	_____	_____	_____
Product C	_____	_____	_____

Comments/Proposed Action _____

_____

_____

_____

_____

_____

_____

Signature _____

Date _____

Fill Out Variance Reports Regularly

Timely information is a lot more valuable than stale information. That's why variance reports are useful: They demand repeated comparison of actual performance against stated goals while this information is still useful.

If the necessary information is not available on a monthly basis or it comes in six weeks after the end of the month, you have a different kind of problem. At the very least, you should have prompt monthly information on budgets, sales, production, and selected variable expenses.

All a variance report can do is to make you aware of a variance. It won't lead you to the cause or tell you what action to take.

If you have carefully identified the standard costs and key variables in your business and have based your projections and budgets on experience and good cost information, the variances will be minimal. Some measures are more sensitive than others. It may be useful to divide costs into those that are controllable, those that might become controllable, and those that cannot be controlled. Your aim is to move as many as possible into the controllable column. Sometimes this can be done simply by keeping a sharp eye on them.

There are several ways to get a handle on which costs need to be more firmly controlled. One is gross dollar amount. Look into any costs over an established dollar amount. Another is fixed versus variable cost analysis. Fixed costs don't need to be scrutinized as often as variable costs, which are more closely associated with sales levels. Another method is percentage deviation. Any variances over 5%, for example, are examined; any over 8% require immediate action.

Take Action as Indicated

A variance report is a guide to action. Get the report each month, study it, think about what the variances imply, then take action. If, for example, sales are down this month, but unit costs are up, find out why. Maybe sales are down because of new competition. Maybe the pricing structure needs adjusting. Perhaps a salesperson is goofing off. Maybe sales were increasing by the end of the month and will level out over the quarter.

All a variance report can do is wave a red flag at you. Once you know what the symptom is, you can look for a cause and a cure. The unseen problems are the ones that can destroy a business.

As with any system, variance reports become rusty after a while. Circumstances change. Cost structures alter, new equipment and competition change the picture. Expenses surge as sales volume increases.

Hence the need to update the system at least annually. Review plans for the coming year, and make adjustments as necessary.

Ratio Analysis Trends Chart

Name	Formula	Month 1	Month 2	Month 3	Comments
Current Ratio	Current Assets/Current Liabilities				
Quick Ratio (Acid Test)	Cash & Mkt. Sec. & Accts. Rec./Current Liabilities				
Debt-to-Worth	Total Debt/Tangible Net Worth				
Cash Earnings Coverage	Net Profit & Depreciation/Current Maturities LTD				
Receivables Turnover	Total Annual Sales/Accounts Receivable				
Days Sales Outstanding	365 Days/Receivables Turnover				
Inventory Turnover	Total Annual Cost of Sales/Inventory				
Days Inventory	365 Days/Inventory Turnover				
Payables Turnover	Total Annual Purchases/Accounts Payable				
Days Payable Outstanding	365 Days/Payables Turnover				
Return on Assets	Pretax Profit/Total Assets				
Return on Investment	Pretax Profit/Tangible Net Worth				
	Pretax Profit/Sales				
	Gross Margin/Sales				
Income Statement Ratios	Annual Sales/Monthly Sales				
	Interest Expense/Sales				

Summary

Variance reports won't take up much of your time. They don't cost much. They don't require a huge front-end investment. And they pay off. If your budgets don't work as well as you'd like them to, try variance reports. By checking performance against budgets monthly, you make sure that the budgets work over the course of a year. This is especially important for a growing company, since growth depletes both liquidity and bankability due to the erosion of ratios. Variance reports won't prevent these problems, but they'll help you diminish their impact.

Action Plan

Financial Controls

- ❏ Acquire cost data. You can control expenses more easily than revenue.
- ❏ Prepare monthly income statements and cash flow projections.
- ❏ Prepare variance reports monthly (or more often).
- ❏ Compare financial and operating ratios, every month, against the standards you have set.
- ❏ Decide how large a variation is acceptable before you act. Take action as indicated.
- ❏ Review your systems periodically, and revise them as needed (usually once a year will be sufficient).

CHAPTER 10

Deviation Analysis

Your cash flow budget, established and tested over time, helps you to consistently observe and control your actual (as opposed to estimated) performance. At least once a month, spend a few hours on looking for significant deviations between your estimated and actual numbers. Deviation analysis provides an early warning system if your business begins to drift from its charted course. Deviations can also be positive, putting the spotlight on opportunities that might have escaped notice.

If you have more than one source of sales, you may benefit from preparing separate budgets for each profit center. This way you can control them better—and find out where your profits are really generated.

Deviation analysis is best performed as soon as current figures are available. Don't wait until the figures become stale. If filling out the forms and spotting the deviations takes more than a few hours, something has gone wrong. (Usually it's the budget, though not necessarily.)

Deviation analysis puts your managerial task into sharp focus; here is a problem, there is an opportunity. As the owner or manager, it is your job to decide what to do. One measure of how well your business is managed is to compare time spent seeking new profit areas to time spent solving last month's problems. You have to solve the problems first.

You'll need a profit-and-loss projection and a cash flow budget. You must also know what expense and income categories are most appropriate for your business. Those indicated in the forms are—at best—a beginning. Customize the form and fit it to your business. Assuming that you have performed these necessary steps, the first part of monthly deviation analysis is simple. Here are five easy steps (see forms on pages 102–105):

1. Enter Actual Figures in Column A

After entering the sales and expense information on the P&L and the cash sales and other cash inflows and disbursements on the cash flow budget, anomalies will begin to appear. With experience, you will notice when sales are changing their complexion—when a slight rise in credit sales begins, the P&L sales will be higher than usual, cash sales lower. The difference may not be great, but it will show clearly.

For expenses and disbursements, the same kind of patterns will develop. If expenses rise, but cash disbursements do not, then you know that your payables are increasing. There may be excellent reasons for this—say, laying in a seasonal inventory or enduring a seasonal shift in your energy bill. But these are matters that you must track; even such obvious matters can slide by.

Both the cash flow and the P&L tell a story and enable you to manage by exception—in other words, focus on problems and opportunities.

2. Enter Budgeted Figures in Column B

If you have not made a P&L budget, the best way to do so is to go back to the projected annual P&L—the basis of your cash flow budget. Most of the items on a projected P&L are based on a combination of: 1. experience, 2. anticipated changes for the next year (preferably documented and carefully reasoned), and 3. industrial averages such as NCR, Robert Morris, and trade figures.

Since the P&L projection is at the center of your business plan, it is a must-do item. Your projected P&L is the numerical expression of the plans you have made for your business. For anyone who wants to achieve profit goals and control the ordinary expenses that bleed profits, time spent careful-ly establishing these projections will be repaid many times over.

Your projected P&L gives annual totals for each item—each product or service line and all expense items. Divide these line totals by 12. This assumes that each month approximately 1/12th of the annual budget will be spent. Expenses such as legal and accounting, insurance, dues, licenses, and fees should be allocated evenly throughout the year. If there is a major seasonal fluctuation or a proposed major asset acquisition (or any major change in your business), adjust your P&L budget to suit the change.

3. Calculate Dollar Amount of Deviation

You need to know the dollar deviation from the budget amounts. Subtract the Actual from the Budgeted (Column A from Column B) to arrive at the change. Enter that figure in Column C. Decide well in advance which deviations are and are not acceptable. Also make notations of acceptable levels or ranges of deviation for future reference.

4. Calculate Percent Deviation, Multiply Result by 100

This is purely mechanical—but it affords a chance to think about each income and expense item, each cash inflow and outflow.

5. Fill in Year-to-Date Forms (Both P&L and Cash Flow)

This step is also mechanical—fill in the columns, keeping a running total by adding this month's figures to last month's year-to-date figures. By doing this, you multiply the effectiveness of your monthly deviation analysis. The monthly forms help identify sharp deviations caused by sudden shifts or unforeseen events. But the slow, subtle trends are apt to slide by the month-by-month analysis; the year-to-date forms highlight these trends.

Up to this point, the review is largely mechanical. It's a simple matter to enter numbers on a form, and the forms could be filled out by your book-keeper. But from here on in, it's your job as owner or manager to use the information. *This cannot be delegated.*

Determine Acceptable Deviation Limits

1. Determine what total or absolute dollar deviation is acceptable.
2. Determine what percentage deviation is acceptable.
3. Decide well in advance what deviations are and are not acceptable.

Compare P&L and Cash Flow

This step has four distinct substeps. Look for:
1. Deviations appearing on both sets of forms,
2. Deviations appearing on just one form,
3. Trends as opposed to spot occurrences, and
4. Deviations that are under your control, and deviations that are not.

Deviations appearing on both sets of forms are clearly red flags. These are (usually) unforeseeable fluctuations, major problem areas, or, if positive, situations you wish to encourage. The principle: Spot the deviation first, then you can find out why it has occurred.

Suppose the deviation is on the P&L but not on the cash flow form. Several

Profit & Loss

Month _____	A: Actual for Month	B: Budget for Month	C: Deviation B – A	D: % Deviation C/B x 100
SALES				
LESS: Cost of Goods				
GROSS PROFIT ON SALES				
OPERATING EXPENSES:				
VARIABLE EXPENSES				
Sales salaries (commissions)				
Advertising				
Miscellaneous variable				
TOTAL VARIABLE EXPENSES				
FIXED EXPENSES				
Utilities				
Salaries				
Payroll taxes & benefits				
Office supplies				
Insurance				
Maintenance & cleaning				
Legal & accounting				
Delivery				
Licenses				
Boxes, paper, etc.				
Telephone				
Miscellaneous				
Depreciation				
Interest				
TOTAL FIXED EXPENSES				
TOTAL OPERATING EXPENSES				
NET PROFIT				
TAX EXPENSES				
NET PROFIT AFTER TAXES				

Cash Flow

Month _____	A: Actual for Month	B: Budget for Month	C: Deviation B – A	D: % Deviation C/B x 100
BEGINNING CASH BALANCE				
ADD: Sales Revenue Other Revenue				
TOTAL AVAILABLE CASH				
DEDUCT: Estimated Disbursements				
Cost of materials				
Variable labor				
Advertising				
Insurance				
Legal & accounting				
Delivery				
Equipment*				
Loan payments				
Mortgage payment				
Property tax expense				
DEDUCT: Fixed Cash Disbursements				
Utilities				
Salaries				
Payroll taxes & benefits				
Office supplies				
Maintenance & cleaning				
Licenses				
Boxes, paper, etc.				
Telephone				
Miscellaneous				
TOTAL DISBURSEMENTS				
ENDING CASH BALANCE				

Calculations: A. Add current month actual to last month's year-to-date analysis.
              B. Add current month budget to last month's year-to-date analysis.

Equipment expense represents actual expenditures made for purchase of equipment.

Profit & Loss

Year-to-Date _____	A: Actual YTD	B: Budget YTD	C: Deviation B – A	D: % Deviation C/B x 100
SALES				
LESS: Cost of Goods				
GROSS PROFIT ON SALES				
OPERATING EXPENSES:				
VARIABLE EXPENSES				
Sales salaries (commissions)				
Advertising				
Miscellaneous variable				
TOTAL VARIABLE EXPENSES				
FIXED EXPENSES				
Utilities				
Salaries				
Payroll taxes & benefits				
Office supplies				
Insurance				
Maintenance & cleaning				
Legal & accounting				
Delivery				
Licenses				
Boxes, paper, etc.				
Telephone				
Miscellaneous				
Depreciation				
Interest				
TOTAL FIXED EXPENSES				
TOTAL OPERATING EXPENSES				
NET PROFIT				
TAX EXPENSES				
NET PROFIT AFTER TAXES				

Deviation Analysis

Cash Flow

Year-to-Date _____	A: Actual YTD	B: Budget YTD	C: Deviation B – A	D: % Deviation C/B x 100
BEGINNING CASH BALANCE				
ADD: Sales Revenue Other Revenue				
TOTAL AVAILABLE CASH				
DEDUCT: Estimated Disbursements				
Cost of materials				
Variable labor				
Advertising				
Insurance				
Legal & accounting				
Delivery				
Equipment*				
Loan payments				
Mortgage payment				
Property tax expense				
DEDUCT: Fixed Cash Disbursements				
Utilities				
Salaries				
Payroll taxes & benefits				
Office supplies				
Maintenance & cleaning				
Licenses				
Boxes, paper, etc.				
Telephone				
Miscellaneous				
TOTAL DISBURSEMENTS				
ENDING CASH BALANCE				

Calculations: A. Add current month actual to last month's year-to-date analysis.
B. Add current month budget to last month's year-to-date analysis.

Equipment expense represents actual expenditures made for purchase of equipment.

possibilities are common—a bill has been forgotten or paid too soon. An expense was unanticipated and will show up on a future cash flow. An expense proved unnecessary and won't appear later. There are any number of possibilities—but if you can track down the cause of the deviation, you will be ahead.

Suppose the deviation shows up in the cash flow but not on the P&L. Again, there are many possible reasons—bills paid too soon or not at all (or never incurred), unexpected purchases, new personnel costs. But by going over each item, including the fixed cash disbursements, the cause will soon be spotlighted. Then you can take action before the problem gets out of hand.

By looking carefully at the monthly and year-to-date forms, you'll spot the trends that may be small each month, yet represent a significant sum over a period of time. Long-range, the goal is to manage your business more profitably; deviation analysis helps cut costs and increases your ability to spot opportunities for new business. Both add to your bottom line. That's one reason it's such a powerful financial troubleshooting tool.

Summary

Deviation analysis is a technique that takes little time and yields excellent results. The mechanical part—recording the information—may be done by any person who is thorough. But the most important parts, such as setting limits to work within and making sure the limits are observed, are your job. The goal is to make your job more manageable. As you practice deviation analysis, you will find that you have more time to improve your company and that you need to spend less time cleaning up yesterday's problems.

Action Plan

Monthly Deviation Analysis

❑ Enter actual monthly figures on deviation analysis forms (both P&L and cash flow).
❑ Enter budgeted figures on both monthly forms (Column B).
❑ Calculate dollar amount of deviation.
❑ Calculate percent deviation. Multiply result by 100.
❑ Fill in year-to-date forms (both P&L and cash flow).
❑ Look for any items (on each form) where the deviation from standards or budgets is significant.
❑ Compare P&L and cash flow.
❑ Determine course of action, implement, and review.

CHAPTER 11

Interim Financial Statement Analysis

You don't have to be a financial guru to benefit from analyzing your company's interim statements. You want to be consistent and look at your monthly statements (income statement and balance sheet) with an eye to changes from one month to the next.

Each month, take 10 figures from the most current financial statements available to you. Calculate 10 simple (arithmetic) ratios and follow them from month to month. Then use the trends and ratios as information to help you make decisions.

Unlike your banker, you won't be concentrating on the so-called "safety" ratios such as "Times Interest Earned" or "Cash Flow/Current Maturities of Long Term Debt." While these are extremely important, their function is to assess the ability of a company, based on the experience of the company's industry, to handle additional debt load.

And unlike an investor in the stock market, you won't be looking for earnings ratios or complicated balance sheet footnotes showing changes in accounting methods that could alter the meaning of the figures. Working with interim statements for operating purposes has a different method.

Interim analysis is not a substitute for the more thorough analyses of financial statements that you do once or twice a year. Its sole purpose is to provide a simple method of putting information gained from interim financial statements into a form that can be used to guide short-term operating decisions.

You may not be using monthly balance sheets and income statements—many executives prefer to rely solely on cash flow budgets and deviation analysis to manage their businesses in the short term. While a cash flow budget is a necessity, and deviation analysis is a nifty method of implementing and using that budget, these tools alone provide only a partial view.

Create Monthly Balance Sheet and Income Statements

Your balance sheet, used in conjunction with your income statement, provides information about ability to meet current obligations (liquidity measures), effectiveness of your sales and collection efforts, asset management, and profitability of current operations. These are obviously handy measures—and they take very little time and effort to generate. Your bookkeeper can produce them within a few days of month's end, as soon as the statements are available. If you have a computerized general ledger system, you can generate interim statements almost instantaneously at any time of the month.

The balance sheet, showing how your company's assets and liabilities were distributed as of the last day of the preceding month, is a snapshot: It freezes the action, shows the results of the operations of the business as of a certain date, and provides a baseline from which to measure changes.

The income statement is a more dynamic indicator of operations. It shows sales, gross margin, and, of course, profits for a specific period. The changes in the income statement show up in the balance sheet as reallocation of assets and liabilities: If the company is making a steady profit, the balance sheet will show it in increased assets and/or reduced liabilities and in increasing net worth.

Since the income statement shows expenses and sales as they occur rather than when the bills are paid or the sales turn into cash, it affords a different kind of measure than the cash flow statement. In many ways the income statement is a less sensitive measure when taken alone, but taken in conjunction with income statements from prior time periods and from industry averages, it helps you identify directions of some trends. When used with the comparable balance sheet, an income statement is even more revealing. In expert hands it can show where money came from and where it went, as well as noncash expenses such as amortization or depreciation.

There are additional reasons why you may need frequent financial statements. Your budgets may be based on the income projections rather than the cash flow projections. The discipline of assembling monthly statements makes you pay more attention to fixed expense control, a phenomenon that many business owners ignore—to their woe. Sales fluctuations are spotted more quickly, as are aberrations in controllable expenses.

Determine Key Ratios and Trends in Your Business

The spreadsheets on pages 114 and 115 provide for the calculation of 10 key ratios, plus room to examine seven key balance sheet items and three key income statement items. Besides these 20 measures, you probably will have other ratios or financial statement items that you want to track. Keep the number reasonable, though—too many "key" measures can be as misleading as none. Suppose, for example, that your business extends a great deal of credit, much of it to questionable accounts. Knowing how many days receivables are outstanding would be helpful—but you would want more detailed information, perhaps broken down in an aging of the receivables, showing the status of accounts receivable of 40 days, 50, 60, 70, 80, 90, and over.

For ordinary monthly operations management, the fewer items to follow, the better. Here are the 10 items you should track.

1. Cash and Near Cash

The availability of highly liquid assets is vital to the survival of most companies. You need cash to pay ongoing expenses including payroll, taxes, and other current liabilities. Changes in these accounts need close attention. You want to minimize idle cash yet maintain liquidity. You may be able to use a cash management system centered on a zero balance checking account or some kind of investment account. Ask your banker.

Excess cash may indicate bills not paid, early payments by your customers, new investment or debt, sale of a fixed asset, or any number of possibilities. Insufficient cash may mean that sales or receivables collection have fallen off, a major asset has been purchased with cash, a bill has been prepaid, suppliers are demanding cash on delivery, or some other problem.

2. Accounts Receivable

While these are close to cash, they can't be used to pay bills unless you collect them, borrow against them, or sell them. Any change in receivables this month affects next month's operating cash flow—assuming standard 30-day terms—so an increase or decrease has serious implications. Forewarned is forearmed. Track your receivables. Receivables rising? Maybe sales are up. Or collection efforts are down. Or the market is shifting toward more extensive use of credit, or sales are being made to a different market segment. Receivables down? This could signal better collections, lowered sales, downturns in the business climate, tightening of credit standards, or higher cash sales.

3. Inventories

These are even further removed from cash. If inventories represent a substantial portion of your company's current assets, this could be a major index of future operating concerns. Lower inventories tell a different story. Perhaps the business has upgraded its inventory management. Perhaps a reorder point was missed, a line dropped, or an unusual order put pressure on the inventory and replacement stock hasn't yet been delivered. Higher inventories could mean a sales slump, careful stockpiling against anticipated production needs, careless ordering, or wise investment against a price rise or shortage.

In and of themselves, inventory levels are merely indications. You need to investigate the root cause of excessively high or excessively low inventory levels.

4. Current Assets and Total Assets

These are more useful for ratio calculation than for operating purposes, although a sudden change in either of these would indicate a need for further examination. Usually the changes in, for instance, a lower inventory will show up as higher cash or receivables, leaving the totals unchanged.

5. Current Liabilities

As these rise and fall monthly, you have to follow them. If they fall, you may be retiring debt or paying bills too swiftly, may have forgotten to place an order, may have missed posting a bill. Or maybe cash flow has improved, enabling you to catch up and get ahead of liabilities, take trade discounts, and lower your costs. The change from normal triggers the question: Why?

Suppose current liabilities are higher this month than last. You may be assuming new debt, ordering additional inventory, or gearing up for higher sales due to seasonality. Awareness of the change triggers your questions.

6. Total Debt

Changes in debt level (other than new debt) are indirectly tied to operations, but since debt is ultimately repaid from operating profit, keep an eye on it. Your banker will be interested in changes in the amount of debt your company carries. Too much debt is dangerous; too little may indicate overly cautious financial management resulting in lower sales and loss of market share.

7. Net Worth

If your business is making money, this tends to rise. If you're losing money on operations, this falls—and since in many ways net worth is an ongoing report card on overall management, you should monitor it closely. Your banker does.

8. Sales

The implications of fluctuations here are obvious. You know that if sales are steadily rising or falling, your cash flow will change predictably. So will the work flow and other operating concerns; inventories will have to be adjusted, personnel hired or laid off, and so on.

However, sales for many businesses are seasonal, and if you don't know the pattern for your business, you could be making unwise decisions.

Sales increases or decreases this month will affect next month's balance sheet—and the balance sheet items have a direct bearing on the level and profitability of sales you can afford. At least quarterly, you and your accountant or treasurer should carefully examine changes in the balance sheet and in sales and expense. Ask for a funds flow statement and an explanation.

But on a monthly basis, your concerns are simpler. What is happening to sales? Are they rising or falling? What will happen next month (to make sure that your operation is ready to meet that sales level)? Why?

9. Gross Margin

Almost as important as the sales figure, the gross margin shows how well operations are being performed.

Gross margin is figured by subtracting the cost of sales from gross sales. Since the cost of sales goes up or down with sales (usually, though not always, with perfect synchrony), the amount of revenue available to meet fixed expenses is governed by this figure. Careless production, for example, will show up as higher cost of sales. Sloppy work flow, careless ordering of raw inventories, and short-term cost problems tend to cluster here.

Rising margins are desirable. Lowered margins aren't—unless there is a good reason for the change, such as increased training costs.

10. Net Profit

The bottom line: If the trend of profits is upward, good. If not, bad. And in either case, changes call for asking why.

However, constant attention to short-term profit is foolish. While you would normally want constant profitability, some costs that affect short-term profits are not that onerous in the long term. Such costs might include new debt service to cover plant and equipment expansion, training costs for new or promoted personnel, or administrative costs to establish a new branch office.

In light of these costs, borrowing from short-term profits to ensure long-term profits can be a good thing.

Ratios

Corresponding to the figures from the financial statements, ratios make relationships in the business more understandable. A ratio is only a shorthand note: They show what's going on according to your books. If your books are accurate portrayals of your business, here are 10 checkpoints to think about.

1. Acid Test, or Quick Ratio: Cash and Near Cash/Current Liabilities

Measures ability to meet current debt, a stringent test since it discounts the value of inventories. The rule of thumb is 1:1. Lower indicates illiquidity. Higher may imply unused funds.

2. Current Ratio: Current Assets/Current Liabilities

Another measure of ability to meet current obligations. Less accurate than the acid test for the very near term, but probably a better measure for six months to a year out, since it contains receivables and inventories as well as cash and near cash. The rule of thumb is 2:1, though this will be affected by seasonality.

3. Receivables Turnover: Sales/Receivables

Measures effectiveness of credit and collection policies. If your ratio is going down, maybe collection efforts are improving, sales are rising, or receivables are being reduced. If going up, sales credit policies may be changing, collection efforts flagging, or sales may have taken a nosedive.

Caution: This ratio depends on when receivables are measured and the seasonality of the business. Careful bookkeeping is also essential. The same applies to inventory turnover: Make sure that the measures are comparable from month to month. Use average receivables (inventories) if you can.

4. Days Receivables: 30/Receivables Turnover

Another way of looking at receivables. Particularly useful in explaining graphically what changes in credit and collection operations do to a business.

5. Inventory Turnover: Cost of Goods Sold/Average Inventory

A measure of how well inventory is managed. Most businesses have a steady inventory turn. Compare your figures from year to year, asking yourself what causes the inevitable fluctuations. Small fluctuations are probably due to the flow of work. If you produce one jumbo jet a year, your inventory picture will be very different from that of a dealer in ripe tomatoes.

6. Days Inventory: 30/Inventory Turnover

Another way of monitoring inventory. This is controlled by your inventory ordering patterns (among other considerations), so be careful in how you interpret it.

7. Gross Margin: Gross Margin/Sales

Permits comparison of margins over months with dissimilar sales. Ideally, this holds pretty steady in good months and bad—but it depends on your business. It can distort fluctuations if sales are erratic.

8. Net Profit: Net Profit/Sales

An overall batting average: The aim is consistency over the long haul, not just short-term stardom.

9. ROI (Return on Investment): Net Profit/Net Worth

Another profitability ratio, best looked at only occasionally, as it tends to magnify short-term shifts in thinly capitalized companies.

10. ROA (Return on Assets): Net Profit/Total Assets

A better profitability measure than ROI. ROA shows how well you are using your assets. However, since profits are a volatile short-term measure, this should also be taken with a grain of salt. The long-term trend is what matters. A large investment in new fixed assets to handle growth will seriously alter this ratio.

All ratios must be taken in context. The reason to look at them on a monthly basis is to make sure that you spot trends as they develop, not afterwards. If you are doing something exceedingly well, you need to know it. And if something is going wrong, better to find out about it sooner than later.

Fill Out Spreadsheets

The next step: Fill out the spreadsheets (see next page). Make copies: You will need several each month to make best use of information generated from them.

First, copy last month's Column B into this month's Column A for all three sections (balance sheet, income statement, ratio analysis). Second, copy this month's figures into Column B. You will have to calculate this month's ratio—but otherwise all you do is copy 20 numbers and fill in the headings.

Income Statement

	A: Last month	B: This month	Change (B – A) $ %	Comments
Net Sales				
Cost of Goods Sold				
Gross Margin				
Operating Expenses				
Net Profit				

Balance Sheet

Cash				
Near Cash				
Accounts Receivable (Net)				
Inventory				
Other				
Total Current Assets				
Fixed Assets				
Total Assets				
Current Liabilities				
Total Liabilities				
Net Worth				

Note Changes

Subtract Column A from Column B. This gives the absolute change to this month from last month—and be sure to indicate the direction of change, positive or negative.

Next, calculate percent change. This will magnify small changes, which can sometimes be helpful.

Finally, fill in the Comments column. If further action is proposed, make a note about who is to do what—and by when. This provides an extremely helpful tool for setting priorities; if you are following the right indicators for your business, this effort will more than pay for itself the first time you use it.

Ratio Analysis Worksheet

	Definition	(A) Last Month	(B) This Month	(B – A) Change	Comments
Acid Test	cash & near cash current liabilities				
Current Ratio	current assets current liabilities				
Receivables Turnover	sales receivables				
Days Receivables	30 receivables turn				
Inventory Turnover	cost of goods sold average inventory				
Days Inventory	30 inventory turn				
Gross Margin	gross margin sales				
Net Profit	net profit sales				
ROI	net profit net worth				
ROA	net profit total assets				

Take Action as Appropriate

One action you should take is to keep the spreadsheets from month to month, as a constant reminder of actions you think should have been taken in the past (or as a record of actions you did take). The cumulative effect of several month's minor improvements in operations can be striking. This is an incremental approach to improving operations, not a quick cure, but it has the advantage of being very controlled.

The spreadsheets will also be helpful when you write your annual business plan and plan strategies for the future, as well as being handy for setting monthly goals.

Ordinarily, based on the experience of people who have followed this kind of management, you will have to fight overreacting at first. If you haven't been following these items on a regular basis, it can be a bit unsettling until you get used to discounting unimportant short-term fluctuations. The trick is to separate the unimportant from the important, and that takes a lot of experience.

As with any management technique, this one works only as well as you make it work. It doesn't solve every problem—but it will help you identify operational problems before they swamp you.

Action Plan

Interim Financial Statement Analysis

❏ Fill out spreadsheets for income statement, balance sheet, and key ratios.
❏ Note changes from month to month, both in direction and in amount. Keep your budget standards in mind.
❏ Take action as appropriate.

CHAPTER 12

Ratio Analysis

F inancial ratios help you get a better handle on your operation, see when things are out of kilter, and set down milestones for the future. And once you get the hang of it, it won't take you more than half an hour a month.

Some common concerns are: Do I have enough working capital? Will I be able to make payroll and the next flock of bills? Is my debt too high? Will I have any difficulty meeting my long-term obligations? Am I using my assets wisely? Is my inventory too large, or does it take too long to turn over? How profitable is my business? Financial ratios help you answer these questions.

Those who use ratio analysis say that business is a new world for them. Life is a lot easier. They can spend more time working on critical areas instead of guessing which ones need attention. Some people say the beauty of financial ratios is that they provide a report card. If you're doing a good job, you know it. If you're not, you know that, too, and you can do something about it. As one recent convert explained, "Ratios are great because they help you know your business—by making you look at everything."

Some businesspeople don't use ratios because they think they're too much trouble. Or because their accountants don't provide them with the information. Or because they never used them in the past, don't think about them, and don't miss them. Others say they're just too busy buying a truck, getting an order out, or taking care of a snafu to worry about the luxury of generating ratios.

The point is that financial ratios are steaks, not bitter pills. They help you to know what you're doing right as well as what you may be doing wrong. What you do right, you can continue doing. What you do wrong, you can work to correct. As your business grows, you can't shoot in the dark. Learn what causes things to work and not work in your business, and you may save yourself hundreds of hours or thousands of dollars.

> ### Flags
>
> **Red:** Off-target negative. A possible problem. Danger. Stop and check on it.
>
> **Yellow:** On target. Keep an eye on it.
>
> **Green:** Off-target positive. A possible strength. Go right ahead.
>
> **Key:** Know WHY your flags are red, yellow, or green. Identify your problems and strengths.

Ratios are numbers formed by comparing one component of your business with another—the ratio expresses the relationship between the two. But a ratio in and of itself is of no value; it must be compared to some standard. Ratio analysis is to running a business as using a compass is to steering a boat. It helps you to determine your direction so you can reach your destination.

Ratios are flags. When you compare your latest financial ratio with a standard (past ratios, industry ratios, or future ratios as goals), you can tell whether you are on or off target. If your latest ratio is very close to the standard, it is a yellow flag. It means, "Not bad, keep your eyes open, and proceed with caution." If your latest ratio is off target in a positive way, it is a green flag. It means, "Good for you, you're doing something well. Know why, and continue." If your ratio is out of whack, it is a red flag. It means, "Danger, stop, and see if anything is wrong."

The process for using financial ratios is easy. Start with your current financial statements. Use them to calculate the financial ratios. These ratios form the basis for important management decisions. Compare the ratios against your standards. Study your red and green flags. Determine their causes. Identify problems and develop solutions. Then, review your new ratios to see how much you've improved.

Thirteen key ratios are used in the financial community, divided into four classes: liquidity, leverage, activity (operations), and profitability.

What the Different Ratios Tell You

Liquidity: How liquid am I? Do I have enough working capital? Not enough? Too much?

Leverage: How much debt to equity do I have? Is this good or bad?

Activity: How efficiently do I use my resources?

Profitability: How profitable am I?

Use Current, Accurate Financial Statements

You'll need your income statement (P&L) and your balance sheet. These should be prepared monthly. If you wait too long, a problem could go undetected for many months. The statements must be timely. And they must be accurate. Inaccurate or corrupt figures are dangerous and misleading.

Balance Sheet = Snapshot (freezes action on a certain day, usually the end of a period)

Income Statement = Motion Picture (tells what happened during a period, normally a year, between the starting date and the ending date, say from January 1 to December 31)

Note: You need both statements to calculate ratios.

Calculate Liquidity Ratios

Liquidity ratios are important because they tell you how much "cushion" you've got before you're in trouble. They measure how well your current assets cover your current obligations. If you can't cover current obligations, then suppliers, creditors, and employees will crowd you until your business begins to shake and crumble.

The problem in projecting cash flow is that it isn't constant throughout the year. It fluctuates. So you've got to have enough of a cushion to cover adverse fluctuations. If your ratios are too low, you could run into a cash flow problem and have trouble meeting payroll and other short-run obligations.

The Quick Ratio, or Acid Test. This sensitive ratio gives a quick, simple reading of your short-term liquidity.

$$\frac{\text{Current Assets} - \text{Inventory}}{\text{Current Liabilities}} = \text{The Acid Test}$$

Suppose your Acid Test is .2:1, the industry average is .7:1, and your goal is .7:1. Red flag. You have a liquidity problem. Better increase sales and cut costs.

An old, successful business warrior told us that over the years he could get a sense of how his business was doing by keying into the variations of his Acid Test. It spotlights approaching liquidity problems. As such, it is a great early warning signal for cash flow problems. Again, he was talking about long-term trend analysis.

The Current Ratio. Inventory is included in the Current Ratio. Since inventory is the least liquid of all assets and can't be instantaneously changed into cash to pay a bill, this ratio is less precise than the Acid Test.

$$\frac{\text{Current Assets}}{\text{Current Obligations}} = \text{Current Ratio}$$

Suppose your Current Ratio is 1.6:1, the industry average 1.8:1, and your goal 2:1. It's not exactly a red flag, but you're not sitting pretty either. Watch things because you're off your goal by 20%. If your inventory makes up most of your current assets, you're in some difficulty because your most liquid assets are in short supply. Current assets include (in order of decreasing liquidity): cash, short-term securities, accounts receivable, and inventory. A ratio of 1.0 would mean that you would have just enough liquidity to cover your obligations. That figure would be okay if there were no business fluctuations. However, since business does fluctuate, sometimes unpredictably, you could be behind the eight ball with the slightest blip if your Current Ratio were 1.0. So it must be high enough to have a cushion (check your industry's standards).

Calculate Leverage Ratios

Leverage ratios measure the relationship between debt, assets, and net worth. How much risk do the creditors bear? A second group of leverage ratios is called coverage ratios—they measure the ability to pay interest expense and other fixed charges annually. They're similar in ways to liquidity ratios. They tell how easily you can pay loan interest. If the cushion is large enough, creditors beam with pleasure because they know they'll get their money back.

We'll look at four leverage ratios: two dealing with debt, assets, and net worth, and two dealing with coverage.

Total Debt to Total Assets. Divide your total liabilities (short- and long-term debt) by your total assets.

$$\frac{\text{Total Debt}}{\text{Total Assets}} = \text{Total Debt to Total Assets}$$

Let's say your Debt to Asset ratio is .8:1 and the industry's is .5:1. Red flag. Your debt is too high. You will probably have difficulty getting bankers to give you more loans. This might be a good time to go in and talk to your banker.

This is a critical ratio that tells whether the balance of risk is on the side of the creditors or owners. If the ratio is high, there is much more debt than equity, which means that additional bank borrowing might be difficult.

Many owners try to get as much of the operation financed by loans as possible, which shifts the risk to the creditors. If owners finance most of the business themselves, the risk is shouldered by the owners.

The greater the ratio, the greater potential profitability during boom periods. However, in bad times, the chance of loss is greater because the equity cushion might not be enough to keep the business going. Boiled down to the nitty gritty, a high leverage means greater profit to owners during good times (their debtors are receiving monthly payback checks and everyone's happy).

But during bad times, it can be disastrous because additional working capital will have to come from equity infusions or personal loans. If owners can't do that, the business collapses. When leverage is high, things are rosy on the upside. But on the downside (when times are bad), things come to a halt twice as fast. Hence, it is critical that your leverage ratio be well-balanced.

Debt to Net Worth. The Debt to Net Worth ratio is a more direct measure of leverage.

$$\frac{\textbf{Total Debt}}{\textbf{Total Net Worth}} = \textbf{Total Debt to Total Net Worth}$$

If your Debt/Worth ratio is 3.9:1, the industry's is 3.5:1, your last was 5.2:1, and your goal is 4:1—green flag. You deserve a pat on the back. Great improvement. Your banker will be pleased. Know what you did so you can keep it up.

Times-Interest-Earned. You can tell how easily you can cover your interest payments with this ratio. You can see how you're doing by comparing it with your standards.

$$\frac{\textbf{Profits before Taxes + Interest}}{\textbf{Interest}} = \textbf{Times-Interest-Earned}$$

Your Times-Interest-Earned ratio is 12:1, your last was 4:1, the industry's is 15:1, your goal is 12:1. Green flag. Not quite the industry average, but another pat on the back. Your earnings are up. Know why and how you did it so you can keep up the good work.

Again, because business is volatile, you must have a large enough cushion to ensure that you can pay your interest. Many loan agreements have a long list of covenants attached. If a covenant is breached, the note or loan holder could bring legal action. Also, if the ratio is too low, you could face difficulty borrowing additional money for an expansion or working capital.

Fixed Charge Coverage. This ratio is similar to the Times-Interest-Earned ratio, but it also includes your lease payments. These days, leasing is an important part of business, and many of us have long-term leases. The monthly lease payment is like an interest payment—it's quasi-debt. If you don't make this payment, it's just as if you don't make your interest payments. Creditors get uneasy. Consequently, you must know how well you're covering all of your fixed costs.

$$\frac{\text{Profit before Taxes} + \text{Interest Charge} + \text{Lease Obligation}}{\text{Interest Charge} + \text{Lease Obligation Coverage}} = \frac{\text{Fixed Charge}}{\text{Coverage}}$$

How about if your Fixed Charge Coverage is 6.2:1, your last was 2.1:1, the industry's is 6.5:1, and your goal is 5.8:1? You're right on target. No red flags.

List Standards for Comparison

By comparing your newly calculated ratios with your last set, with other firms like yours in the industry, and with ratios you've established as goals, you can get a handle on how you're doing.

Where do you get them? Pick internal ratios off your financial sheets. Calculate your projected ratio goals once a year, based on what's happening in your operation and the economy, as well as how you feel about what's coming up. You can get industry ratios from many sources, including Dun and Bradstreet, Robert Morris Associates, and trade associations.

What you want are ratios for your industry, in your size and location, monthly (if possible), and as inexpensively as possible. Industry trends are also useful. Pick the ratios from the trade sources and list them on your comparison sheet (see the Ratio Analysis Worksheet, page 115). List the ratios from your last set of financial statements (last review). Plug in your projected goals. This provides everything you need to make your analysis. Look at your three standards. Compare your new ratios with them. Note on the form the ratios that are way off target either negatively (red flag) or positively (green flag).

Pinpoint Liquidity or Leverage Problems

This is the second most important part of the analysis. After reviewing your flags, study the red flags. Check for problems and analyze them as closely as you can. Remember, a problem well identified is almost solved.

Study your green flags. Why are your ratios so good? What is it you're doing well? Try to identify it as well as you can. Knowing what you're doing well is as important as knowing what you're doing poorly.

Develop a Plan and Act on It

Planning should include correcting problems as well as maintaining your strengths. This is the most important step of the analysis. Take action! Don't wait. Time works against you when you have a problem. And if you don't fortify your strengths, they may wither. Transforming knowledge into action is a major hurdle. Act and check the results of your action by seeing how your ratios have changed at your next review session.

Once you have a fix on liquidity and leverage ratios—and an action plan for responding to them—you can turn to the activity and profitability ratios. Activity ratios, sometimes called productivity or operating ratios, answer the question: How efficiently do I use my resources (inventory, accounts receivable, tangible fixed assets, and total assets)? Profitability ratios are your overall report card. They answer the questions: How profitable is my business? How effectively do I manage it?

Calculate Activity Ratios

Activity ratios are an essential step toward improving your operating efficiency. The four activity ratios are: Inventory Turnover, Receivables to Sales, Fixed Asset Turnover, and Total Assets Turnover.

Inventory Turnover. Your Inventory Turnover ratio is a delicate one—it helps you achieve the right balance between overstocking and understocking, which is a fine line, to be sure. If you're overstocked, you're paying interest on working capital as well as paying for products. Don't pay double duty. If

---

How to Compare Your Ratios with Your Standards

1. Shoot for the **standard**.

2. If you're off, notice the **trend**. Is it up or down? Is this good or bad?

3. Notice the **absolute deviation**. Is it more than 20%, 30%, or 40% off target? (This percentage depends on the ratio.) Develop your ability to judge how much a deviation is off and when you should take action.

4. Compare ratios of **similar situations**. You wouldn't compare the time of an adult man with the time of a young boy for running the mile. Make sure that the firms you are comparing your company with are the same size, product line and, if possible, region.

5. Watch out for **seasonal differences**.

you're understocked, you could have stock-outs, which could give your business a bad image.

Your Inventory Turnover ratio helps you to walk the tightrope between oversupply and undersupply, while suppliers, customers, and creditors tug you in all directions.

$$\frac{\text{Sales}}{\text{Inventory}} = \text{Inventory Turnover}$$

Banker Perspectives

	How Bankers View Liquidity	How Bankers View Leverage
Low	If chronic, this is often evidence of mismanagement. If your firm were properly managed, you'd have planned for working capital. Often associated with last-minute, or "Friday night," financing.	This is a very conservative position. With this kind of leverage, bankers are apt to view your credit demands favorably.
Average	Prima facie evidence of good management. You are using your current assets profitably. When you're customarily in the middle, your banker feels comfortable. No one's going to get concerned.	If your leverage compares favorably with other businesses of your kind and size, bankers are likely to provide some credit, because they feel you aren't being pinched by too high a debt load, and you are showing ability to use your resources.
High	Some bankers love it. It's your most conservative position. However, some feel that you're not using your assets hard enough and are holding too many liquid assets.	If you carry more debt than average, bankers are normally unwilling to lend more unless you can show them extremely good reasons. You may be put on a short-term payout as soon as possible. Any excess liquidity will be called on to retire debt.

When you compare your ratio with your standards, note the deviations. Any large deviation (high or low) in a balancing ratio, such as your Inventory Turnover, is a red flag. You can't go too far in either direction and maintain your balance.

Too low a turnover ratio means your inventory is too large: It's not turning over fast enough. Not only is your inventory costing you extra, but it could indicate theft or old or spoiled stock. It alerts you to poor buying practices and to buying in uneconomical quantities. Some owners or managers buy inventory by the truckload because they're getting a discount, without taking into account the carrying cost.

Too high a turnover ratio means your inventory is too small; it raises the specter of a host of possible problems that may not be immediately apparent: poor buying practices, illiquidity, insufficient profits, or stock-outs.

> ### Implications of Inventory Turnover Ratio
>
> **Too Low:**
> - ☐ Inventory too large
> - ☐ Poor buying practices
> - ☐ Underutilization of working capital
> - ☐ Extra carrying costs chewing into profits
> - ☐ Possible theft
> - ☐ Possible spoiled or outmoded stock
>
> **Too High:**
> - ☐ Inventory too small
> - ☐ Examine the size of your order; improve your purchasing techniques
> - ☐ Improve your marketing
>
> **To reduce:**
> - ☐ Order in more economic lots
> - ☐ Sell off some fixed assets to get cash for inventory
> - ☐ Cut costs
> - ☐ Raise prices

Two things you should keep in mind when comparing sales with inventory are price versus cost and seasonality. Sales are valued by selling price, inventory by cost. Use the cost of goods sold in place of sales to give a purer figure, but check to see how your external standard of comparison has been calculated. If it used price for sales, use price; if cost, use your cost of goods sold. Remember, too, that inventory is seasonal. When comparing your recent ratio with the industry standard, remember that the industry may not reflect seasonal differences. To make your ratio purer, you might have to take an average of your inventory over some set period. Use your judgment here.

Receivables to Sales and Average Collection Period. Your credit policy is one of your important marketing decisions. If your credit is too tight, you lose sales; if too liberal, your carrying costs are high. You must collect receivables within a reasonable time for them to remain a liquid asset. The Receivables to Sales ratio measures the amount of accounts receivable in relation to sales.

Ratio Combinations		Probable Credit Implications
Liquidity	Leverage	
Low	*Low*	Can usually borrow to satisfy short-term working capital needs, put on a long-term payout basis.
Low	*Average*	May find it difficult to get a short-term loan to relieve illiquidity.
Low	*High*	Worst case. Forget it. Bankers see such companies as overborrowed, running out of money, and mismanaged. Borrowing would be extremely unlikely.
Average	*Low*	Highly desirable. Banks see you as able to handle additional debt, especially long-term.
Average	*Average*	Your most profitable position, as both resources and credit are being handled well. Proceed with caution, but a good bet. Some credit capacity and, in a crunch, your banker would usually bail you out.
Average	*High*	May get some short-term financing. No long-term, as debt load is too great.
High	*Low*	The best bet from the bank's position but, operationally, this may be too conservative. You will probably be able to get both short- and long-term financing.
High	*Average*	A good position. Bankers will help you. Use your cash to reduce your long-term debt and become even more appealing to credit grantors.
High	*High*	Not a good position. Chances are poor of getting a loan. Use some of your idle cash to reduce your leverage.

Ratio Analysis Worksheet

Liquidity & Leverage	Future: Projected Goals	External: Industry Averages	Internal: Your Last Ratios	Your New Ratios	Red and Green Flags	Action Taken by/Date
Acid Test						
Current						
Debt/Assets						
Debt/Net Worth						
Times-Interest-Earned						
Fixed Charge Coverage						

$$\frac{\text{Receivables}}{\text{Net Sales}} = \text{Receivables to Sales}$$

Receivables to Sales x 365 = Average Collection Period

When measured against the standards, this ratio tells whether your receivables are high, on target, or low. If high, it might mean that your credit policy is too liberal, your collection method lax, or possibly both. If low, perhaps your credit policy is too stringent, your collection procedure too harsh, or both.

The Average Collection Period is calculated by multiplying your Receivables to Sales ratio by 365, the number of days in a year. This gives your average collection period.

For example, let's suppose sales are $350,000 and receivables are $54,000. Let's calculate the ratios and look at them.

$$\frac{\$54,000}{\$350,000} = .15 = \text{Receivables to Sales}$$

0.15 x 365 = 55 days = Average Collection Period

If you find that your collection period is 55 days, the industry's is 36, and your goal was 38, you know you have to take corrective measures. Your credit policy is too liberal, your collection procedure too lax, or both.

Industry averages for Receivables to Sales and Average Collection Period ratios indicate the balance that's been found in similar businesses.

Again—it's a high-wire balancing act. Too high or too low a ratio is no good.

Fixed Asset Turnover. This important ratio measures the utilization of plant and equipment. It tells how well your firm is using fixed assets relative to other firms in the industry. If the ratio is low, think twice before making new capital investments.

$$\frac{\text{Sales}}{\text{Net Fixed Assets}} = \text{Fixed Asset Turnover}$$

Suppose your ratio is 2.3, your last was 2.5, the industry's is 5.0, and your goal is 5.2. Red flag. You aren't using your plant and equipment to their full capacity. You might consider selling off some underutilized plant and equipment, trying to increase sales, or both.

Total Assets Turnover Ratio. This activity ratio measures the turnover of all of your firm's assets. It is calculated by dividing sales by total assets. Total assets equal plant and equipment plus current assets. This ratio measures whether your firm is generating enough business for its asset investment.

$$\frac{\text{Sales}}{\text{Total Assets}} = \text{Total Assets Turnover}$$

Suppose your ratio is 1.5, your last one was 1.4, the industry average is 2.1, and your goal is 2.0. Red flag. You're well below the external standards and goals. Your company is not generating a sufficient volume for the asset size. Sales should be increased, some assets disposed of, or both.

An asset turnover ratio that's too low is not always bad. It could indicate a wise investment during inflationary periods—because your assets rise in value with inflation, while your debts decrease in value.

However, it could indicate extravagant spending. You can have the biggest, best, and most expensive in office, plant, and equipment, but only if you have the sales to carry them.

Another Balancing Act— Your Credit Policy

No Credit at All	vs.	Generous Credit
No receivables		Very high sales
No carrying costs		Lots of customers
No cost collection		

But—	But—
Lowered sales	High carrying costs
	High collection costs
	Skyrocketing bad debt expense

Key point: You want a policy that balances potential sales and costs.

Calculate Profitability Ratios

Profitability ratios are easy to calculate using your financial statements and are almost impossible to ignore. They answer the bottom-line question: How are we doing? Take a hard look at them. They tell you how much money you made on your investment—whether the sky is clear and blue or whether it's falling. Profitability ratios are your overall report card.

There are three ways of measuring profitability: profit margin against sales, against total assets, and against net worth. The three ratios are: Profit Margin on Sales, Return on Total Assets (or ROI), and Return on Net Worth.

Profitability is the net result of a large number of business decisions, so these ratios tell how well you manage your business, from sales and marketing operations to asset and money management.

Aging Schedule

This schedule breaks down receivables according to how long they've been outstanding. For example:

Age of Accounts (Days)	Total Value of Receivables (Percent)
0-20	6
21-30	8
31-45	26
46-60	20
61-90	20
Over 90	20

The 55-day collection period looks bad in comparison with the industry average. The aging schedule shows the business having serious collection problems with some accounts. If the terms are net 30, 86% are overdue, half for more than two months. Only a few pay promptly; many are very old. The aging schedule shows that the average account has been outstanding for 55 days; a full 20% are more than three months old!

Remember, an average doesn't tell you the range, and the oldest receivables are the ones to worry about.

Profit Margin on Sales. The profit margin on sales, calculated by dividing net income after taxes by sales, gives the profit per dollar of sales. If the ratio is low, it means your prices are too low, costs are relatively high, or both.

This ratio is informative, but it can be misleading. If you have more than one product, you should consult your accountant, banker, or consultant to help you develop a system for determining product line profitability. It's critical to know overhead, depreciation, sales costs, and so on by product line. Without this knowledge, you could have several products that are cutting into your profits and not know about it.

$$\frac{\text{Net Profit after Taxes}}{\text{Sales}} = \text{Profit Margin on Sales}$$

Suppose your ratio is .04, your last was .035, the industry average is .05, and your goal is .05. Red flag. You're off by 20%. You probably should explore raising your prices, cutting costs, or both.

Return on Total Assets. This popular ratio, better known as your Return on Investment (ROI), measures the return on the total investment in your business. It includes debt plus equity investment. This ratio can fluctuate widely if you have a narrow asset base, such as in wholesaling. Therefore, you must take into account the kind of business you are in.

$$\frac{\text{Net Profit after Taxes}}{\text{Total Assets}} = \text{ROI}$$

Suppose your last ratio was .06, or 6%, the one before that was 5%, the industry average is 10%, and your goal is 9.5%. Definite red flag. Your firm is off from the industry average by 40%. Try to increase your profit margin and turn over your total assets more quickly.

Return on Net Worth. This last important ratio measures the rate of return on the owner's investment. It is a more direct measure of profitability because the asset base isn't taken into account. Look at profitability over a longer time frame, perhaps on a yearly basis, to smooth out short-term fluctuations. This ratio doesn't include return on debt, just equity.

$$\frac{\text{Net Profit after Taxes}}{\text{Net Worth}} = \text{Return on Net Worth}$$

If your last Return on Net Worth ratio was 14%, the one before that 13.5%, the industry's is 15%, and your goal is 14%, bull's-eye—you're right on target.

Use Industry Ratios as Standards

Using your financing sheets (P&L and balance sheet), calculate your activity and profitability ratios, and list them on the comparison form. (See Ratio Analysis Worksheet on the next page.) Using the trade journals common to your business and standard financial data sources, such as Dun & Bradstreet and Robert Morris Associates, pick out industry averages for businesses of your type and size, and list them on the form. Finally, plug in your projected ratios (goals). These are your standards for comparison, and they will provide you with everything you need to make your analysis.

Ratio Analysis Worksheet

Activity Ratios	Future: Projected Goals	External: Industry Averages	Internal: Your Last Ratios	Your New Ratios	Red and Green Flags	Action Taken by/Date
Inventory Turnover						
Receivables to Sales						
Average Collection Period						
Fixed Asset Turnover						
Total Asset Turnover						
Profit Margin on Sales						
Net Profit after Taxes (ROI)						
Return on Net Worth						

Compare Ratios with Standards

Look at your new ratios in comparison to the three standards (*see box*). Think about any deviation—are there problems? Opportunities?

Studying your deviations is the second most important part of the analysis. Check them over carefully. Think about them. See if you have either problems or opportunities. If problems, analyze them as thoroughly as possible with your staff. Ferret out the causes. Remember, a problem well-identified is almost solved. Are there any favorable deviations that indicate opportunities? Knowing what you're doing well is as important as knowing what you're doing poorly.

Having determined these causes, you are now armed with powerful ammunition that can help you become more successful.

> **Three Standards Used in Ratio Comparison**
>
> **Internal**
> Last period's ratios
>
> **External**
> Ratios of similar businesses within the industry
>
> **Goals**
> Projected ratios

Develop a Plan of Action

Transforming knowledge into action is the toughest and most important step of the analysis. Take action! If you don't correct your problems, the consequences will be serious. Likewise, if you don't take advantage of opportunities, they will wither on the vine. If you don't move from the stage of knowing to the stage of doing, you will get nowhere.

Develop a well-designed action plan to solve your problems and fortify your strengths. Monitor your actions by checking the ratios at your next review period. Are you moving in the right direction? Is your plan paying off? Do you need to change it? By constantly monitoring your ratios as they change over time (trend analysis), you can tell if your business decisions are appropriate.

Summary

Ratio analysis helps you to make a wide range of decisions, both short-range ones, such as whether to raise a price or borrow more working capital, and long-range ones, such as whether to expand. You can learn a great deal about your liquidity, ability to obtain more debt capital, inventory, credit policy and collection procedures, plant utilization, and profitability. Armed with this information, you'll be able to speak knowledgeably with creditors and investors alike, in bad times as well as good.

Most business owners, even those with math anxiety, are surprised at how easy ratios are to use, how much more they understand about their business, and how much better they are able to manage their business.

Try them. You'll be happy you did.

Action Plan

Ratio Analysis

❏ Calculate liquidity, leverage, activity, and profitability ratios. Enter them on their respective worksheets so you can measure them against standards (industry or your own).

❏ Determine causes of problems or opportunities that are spotlighted by your ratio analysis. Look for trends as well as absolute differences.

❏ Develop a plan and take action. Assign responsibility; measure results. Review and note changes over time.

CHAPTER 13

Credit and Collections

C redit and collection policies are difficult to establish since they are tied so closely to cash flow and sales problems. Easier credit terms tend to increase sales, though often at the cost of lower profits if the sales don't turn to cash on time. Tighter credit requirements, on the other hand, are apt to result in fewer sales—and often at the cost of additional profits from those fringe accounts that turn out to be good (although slow) payers.

Set Credit Objectives

Credit policies need to be directed toward some goal. Otherwise selecting the most appropriate type of credit to offer becomes a game of chance, with the concomitant risks of improper credit, needless credit, and avoidable bad-debt/cash flow losses.

Why extend credit at all? Look to your business goals. Credit objectives should be derived from your wider business objectives. For example, if you are attempting to penetrate new markets, your credit policy would reflect the importance of acquiring new customers no matter how marginal their credit rating might be. If your marketing decision is to limit the number of customers due to a limited number of account representatives or insufficient production capacity, you would probably set more stringent credit requirements. By limiting credit to only the best risks, you would maximize profits.

You cannot establish the best credit policies for your business until you are clear on what objectives these policies are intended to achieve. You cannot set rational credit objectives unless you know where your business is headed. There are factors affecting credit objectives beyond marketing decisions, too. If your business does not have to extend credit at all—an unusual situation these days—your credit objectives might be to extend no credit at all except under the most compelling circumstances, such as a major customer requesting special accommodation.

The ability of credit departments to make large numbers of credit judgments is also a factor. This has obvious implications for credit policies. You might wish to establish a limit to the number of customers to whom credit should be extended. In the next section we raise the basic question of how much credit you can afford to extend. If you have severe cash flow problems, you may find that you cannot afford to extend credit to anyone.

Ask yourself the following questions:

1. Why should we extend credit?
2. What do we hope to achieve by extending credit (stated in terms of dollars of additional sales, dollars of additional profit, number of customers)?
3. What has our credit policy achieved in the past? This is particularly difficult to answer if records make it difficult to distinguish credit sales from cash sales.
4. What would we ideally achieve by changing our credit policies?
5. What changes in credit policies would lead to these desired goals?

If your current methods have been paying off, then change them hesitantly, if at all. A system that has worked in the past and has no glaring faults is certainly a safer route to follow than any new set of procedures. Bear in mind that any change in credit policy is going to result in difficulties in the sales and credit departments. People develop habits that are hard to change. However, if you ask yourself the set of questions raised above and find that there is good reason to question the effectiveness of your current credit policies, then institute new procedures that will achieve your credit objectives.

The more precise you can make your objectives, the better. If your objective is increased dollar sales, how many dollars? When? How many customers does that represent? Make these numbers as specific as possible and ask yourself if these numbers are attainable in the time allotted.

Determine Your Credit Capacity

When you extend credit, you are in essence making an unsecured loan to your customers. The basic question is: Can I afford to extend this credit?

To get a rough fix on the amount of credit you extend to your customers, look at your accounts receivable and compare the total with the amount of short-term bank debt you carry. If you extend more credit than your business can afford, your short-term bank debt will be high relative to the current level of receivables. Look to industry or trade averages to compare performance with your competitors. Ask your banker and accountant. Borrowing from a bank at current interest rates to support slow-paying customers is a sure route to disaster, unless (a) your margins—including reserves for bad debt—are high and (b) you know the costs and can accept them.

Short-term debt may be high for other reasons—inventory, bridge financing, or other legitimate short-term needs. If, however, you constantly have to borrow against receivables, you should review your credit policies with your banker.

The amount of credit you can afford to extend is directly related to your cash flow. Before you extend credit, ask: What will the impact of delayed receipt of funds be on our ability to pay our own bills? If your cash flow is strong enough to permit extending more credit, then perhaps you should consider relaxing credit restrictions, which creates more accounts receivable. If it is a constant struggle to meet fixed payments, then any way you can accelerate cash flow—which includes turning accounts receivable into cash faster—should be vigorously pursued. Tighter credit restrictions will ordinarily accelerate cash flow even though it will reduce total dollar volume.

Beware of the Hidden Costs of Extending Credit

Credit is expensive—to you as a creditor and to the person or business you are extending credit to. Some of the costs are obvious: interest charges to carry accounts receivable, discounts (whether taken or not), and the cost of maintaining a credit and collection department.

Some costs are more subtle. A customer who is past due will often go elsewhere—and pay cash. The strain of worrying about your own cash flow, aggravated by slow-paying customers, can be a major problem. Opportunity costs (in missed sales, missed opportunities and chances) can occur due to preoccupation with avoidable problems.

To calculate the direct cost of past-due accounts, add up all of those accounts receivable over term. They represent money tied up in funding your customers. It amounts to an interest-free loan—unless you charge and collect for the privilege. The 2% finance charge on past-due accounts offsets your cost of working capital and places the cost where it belongs. If you do not follow this standard practice, you incur unnecessary costs.

Establish and Follow Credit Checking Procedures

The best time to improve collection procedures is before any credit is granted. What do you need to know? To extend credit, you must know your customers. Some of the principal pieces of knowledge can best be ascertained through your banker. If you tell your bank what credit information you need and why you need it, the bank will ordinarily provide the information. A standard credit information form is available from your bank. Adapt it to suit your needs.

Your purpose in performing a credit check on *all* your customers, not just on your new ones, is to know how much credit those customers can realistically afford to use.

A standard business credit checklist includes references (see "Credit Checklist" on opposite page). It does you little good to have the references if you don't check into them. Credit checks are normal business procedure, and most businesspeople will be glad to help.

Credit managers divide customers and prospects into four groups: prime customers who provide full operating profits by paying within terms or take discounts, good (70% to 80% of operating profit), average (50% of operating profit), and other (who expose you to significant delinquency rates and bad debt losses). Naturally, you should sell to as many prime and good customers as possible. Check credit in advance to identify these desirable customers. Businesses, like people, tend to follow behavior patterns.

Some of the information to get before extending credit includes number of employees, name of bank, length of time in business, references from three or more vendors, and the names of principals. For any customer, old or new, you should ask for a credit application. Honest prospective customers will understand the need for credit investigations and will not object.

A surprisingly large number of credit decisions are made irrationally. All of us have hunches and intuitions—but credit experts know that people and businesses that have been poor credit risks in the past will continue to be poor credit risks in the future. You can always ask a prospect to explain a negative credit report. You may wish to extend credit in spite of a recent bankruptcy or in the teeth of all rational advice, but at least you will be doing so knowingly and will not be extending credit on whim. If you find that your judgment of creditworthiness is good, follow it. If you find it is not or have questions about how good your judgment is, then follow the book.

Manage Accounts Receivable by Carefully Allocating Credit

Now you have allocated each account, present or prospective, to one of the four categories of credit. The actual mix of the credit you extend—that is, how many dollars you can afford to extend to each category—can be determined by a combination of calculation and experience. Any standard textbook on financial management will help you determine what kind of profit you can expect from selling on credit to each of these various categories.

Many businesses find it extremely profitable to sell to poor credit risks. For

Credit Checklist

Customer name:_____

Date:_____

1. D&B rating:_____

2. Trade references*:_____
Talked to:_____
A. Account open since:_____
B. Last sale:_____
C. Terms:_____
D. High credit:_____
E. Amount owing:_____
F. Amount past due:_____
G. Pays within:_____
Comments:_____
_____
_____

Trade references*: _____
Talked to:_____
A. Account open since: _____
B. Last sale:_____
C. Terms:_____
D. High credit: _____
E. Amount owing:_____
F. Amount past due:_____
G. Pays within:_____
Comments:_____
_____
_____

3. Bank reference: _____
Branch:_____
Officer's name:_____
A. Checking account since:_____
B. Average high: _____
C. Is it a satisfactory account?_____
D. High credit: _____
E. Payment history: _____
Comments: _____
_____

* Check at least two references.

those in the "other" category, significant bad-debt losses can be anticipated, and slow payment is the norm. Such customers frequently cannot get credit and thus are willing to pay a higher price. If the premium they pay for your goods or services outweighs the risk—if you can make money on this group even after absorbing losses for bad debts and increased collection expenses—then it makes good business sense to extend credit to this market. A company that sells to lower categories of credit risks must be structured to handle the problems such a market entails. If your customers tend to be slow paying, then your business should reflect that and so should your credit and collection procedures.

The basic information you need to manage your accounts receivable is gained by aging your receivables, which means listing your accounts receivable by due dates: Current, 30 days, 60 days, and over 60 days (for example). If you sell on 30-day terms, but your customers pay on 60-day terms, and nothing you do can get them to pay faster, you should consider reevaluating your credit procedures. If you extend 30-day terms and your customers pay within 40 days, you are doing a good job.

To determine the average collection period for your credit sales, divide the dollar total of your annual credit sales by 365. This gives a daily credit sale figure. Divide your total accounts receivable (from your latest monthly financial statement) by the daily credit sales figure; this yields your collection period expressed in days.

Accounts Receivable as Days' Sales

Expressing accounts receivables as days' sales should be included as an analytic technique for comparing company performance against industry standards. This will help you decide when your business might begin to have a credit and collection problem.

As an example, in the medical industry a 60- to 62-day collection period is the norm. A medical laboratory that has averaged 59.5 days—a superior performance—might decide to institute changed procedures if its average rises to 61 days, even though that is standard for the industry. Another laboratory might be thrilled to hit 61 days. If its previous performance had been 68 days, the improvement in collection performance would be significant.

It is very important that both the average and the trend for the business be considered. If the collection period is becoming longer and no other reason can be cited (such as a local economic slump), then the increase is a clear warning to management that collection and credit procedures need review.

Expressing averages in days' sales offers another, lesser benefit: They are easily visualized. This can make a difference—especially if the changes are slight in terms of percentages but amount to a day or more of sales. Once your employees can visualize what slackening standards can do, they will make the necessary adjustments in their behavior.

Annual credit sales ÷ 365
= Daily credit sales

Receivables ÷ Daily credit sales
= Collection period in days

The collection period should be no more than one third greater than your net selling terms.

Managing accounts receivable depends on accurate and timely information. Once you know what accounts are outstanding and how much they owe—and whether or not they are current—you should also know, for your own peace of mind, the customary payment practices of those customers, particularly those who owe you large amounts of money. You must closely monitor any potentially dangerous account, but unless you are familiar with these accounts, you increase risk of bad-debt losses. Visit your customers (if possible). Make sure you have current and accurate financial information on them. Keep track of any sudden, unexpected changes in purchasing patterns, bank of deposit, personnel, or suppliers. Periodically review credit limits. Ask for new credit applications from all customers annually.

Credit Check

Date: _____

To: _____

Address: _____

City & State: _____

Kindly provide credit information regarding the following account.

LEDGER FACTS

Sold since: _____

To: _____

Terms: _____

Highest recent credit $ _____

Amount now owing $ _____

Amount past due $ _____

☐ satisfactory ☐ unsatisfactory

MANNER OF PAYMENT

Discounts: _____

Pays when due: _____

Days slow: _____

We will be glad to reciprocate.

Signed _____

Establish and Apply Collection Procedures

Your collection procedures should be firm, consistent, and courteous. Think how you would like to be treated if, for reasons beyond your control, you couldn't pay a bill. Always allow your customer to save face.

Conventional business practice used to call for a series of polite letters beginning the day after an account became delinquent.

That collection procedure no longer works. The day an account becomes overdue (Day 30 if your terms are 30 days), send a reminder letter and call up the customer. Identify the person who is responsible for paying your invoice and ask politely but firmly for payment. This may take some doing, particularly if you are dealing with the payables department of a large company. Some companies find that some of their biggest customers "lose the invoice" regularly no matter what they do. Ask for reasons for nonpayment if necessary, but in all cases try to get a promise to pay a fixed amount on a given date. The form below should be filled out for every collection call. It provides hard information for future calls and also helps if you are forced into litigation.

If your polite letter and phone call do not produce almost immediate results, call again. Most people want to pay their bills—so do most businesses. By making sure that you know the person responsible for paying your account, you will move to the head of the line labeled "those to be paid." Depending on your business and depending on the importance of the customer to you, your next step will vary. The combination of letter and telephone call is difficult to top. You may wish to restrict credit until an account

Collections

Name:_____

Telephone:_____

Spoke to:_____

Title:_____

Subject:_____

Date: _____

Time: _____

Initials: _____

☐ No answer ☐ Not available

☐ Requested info ☐ Requested proof of delivery

☐ Order never received ☐ Payment previously sent

☐ Will send check ☐ Merchandise returned

☐ Duplicate billing ☐ Payment being held

Comments:_____

_____

_____

Returned call:_____

Follow-up: _____

is made current. If so, put a note in the customer's file. You may wish to put a customer on C.O.D. terms, adding a portion of the past-due debt. You may wish to set up partial payment plans, take notes or personal guarantees from the principals of the business, charge interest on the unpaid balance, or use a combination of these techniques.

Some companies find overnight or express delivery letters effective. It is hard to ignore a letter marked "urgent" and addressed to a specific individual, even in the largest corporation.

Collection agencies are a useful intermediary. They can be more aggressive. As experts that specialize in collecting debts, they can help you avoid future credit difficulties. Most reputable collection agencies use a sliding scale based on the amount of money involved and the kind of industry. A fee of 30% to 50% of the amount collected is a reasonable range. Check with your bank and trade or professional association for the best collection agency for your business.

Collection Techniques to Avoid

1. Late-payment charges are often ignored, they don't speed up collections, and they can be hard to enforce.

2. If early payment discounts are offered (such as 2%/10 days), some customers take the discount and still pay in 30 to 60 days.

3. Collection agencies should be considered a last resort. They take a big percentage and often alienate customers.

4. Going to court with a deadbeat may result in a countersuit that costs much more to resolve than the delinquent bill.

5. Even the most reliable credit reports can be misinterpreted, resulting in doing business with bad credit risks or avoiding businesses with potentially good customers.

Most importantly, do not make any threats that you do not intend to follow through on. If you say, "pay within 10 days or the collection agency will be after you," make sure that the collection agency will be after the delinquent client.

Past-due accounts present a number of problems. You don't want to offend a good customer who is experiencing temporary difficulties. On the other hand, you don't want to subsidize someone who is sliding into bankruptcy. Know your customers as well as possible, communicate with them, and use your common sense. You will be able to help good customers while avoiding increased risks. If you suddenly begin to receive postdated or unsigned checks from a customer, or if the size of orders fluctuates greatly or unexpectedly, you may have a customer headed for trouble. Some credit experts say that you should note what bank a check is drawn on—a new bank may indicate a change in circumstances. In any case, the better you know your customer, the less likely you are to be hung up.

Review and Change Policies as Needed

Once you have established your credit and collection policies and have put them into effect, you have to monitor them. Whenever you implement a new policy, you will meet with resistance. Sometimes this resistance is appropriate. By reviewing the impact of your policies—checking to see whether collection periods are strictly observed and profits up—you may find that the old policies are actually the best for your business.

More likely you will find that by focusing attention on credit and collection procedures, performance will improve for a time whether or not any policies are changed. You should review any changed policy after three months. You may wish to change policies again. You may wish to leave them in place, but in any case you will be doing so for rational reasons. Ask yourself:

- Are the credit objectives we set earlier being attained?
- Has the credit capacity of the business changed?
- Should the credit policies be changed again?
- Should you aim for more "average" or "other" customers, even though the bad-debt risk is higher?
- Have bad-debt losses and delinquency rates decreased in dollars or in numbers?

Summary

Aim for a careful balance: Enough credit to increase sales and profitability, not too much to hurt cash flow. Careful use of credit as a sales and marketing tool will increase sales and profits. Such use is based on timely and accurate information: How good is this credit? How will it be paid—and how soon will you be paid if the customer gets into financial trouble?

Action Plan

Credit and Collections

❏ Set credit objectives. What do you want your credit policies to achieve—in specific measurable terms?

❏ How much credit can your company afford to offer?

❏ Categorize customers and prospects by credit categories.

❏ Allocate credit on a customer-by-customer basis.

❏ Monitor average collection period to measure impact of policies.

❏ Establish and follow standard collection practices. Document all customer contacts. Full notes help to resolve disputes in your favor.

CHAPTER 14

Collection: Dealing with Past-Due Accounts

Nobody enjoys pursuing deadbeats who won't pay their bills. There is no joy in seeking payment from persons who want to pay but for various reasons are unable to pay now. But these unpleasant tasks are a fact of business life. A clear credit and collection policy (see Chapter 13) will go far to minimize the need for collection practices, but it won't obviate the need entirely.

Introduction

When does the average business develop procedures for the collection of accounts? Unfortunately, too often—too late. Though new firms recognize the necessity of tackling other specifics of business operations before they open their doors, the idea of problems in billing and collecting, especially delinquent accounts, is avoided like the plague. We always hope it's a predicament that will never come to pass in our business.

Thus, once the problem of a past-due account finally arises with a seriousness that defies further ignoring, it is already a mess. Perhaps the customer in question has shown signs of becoming delinquent for months. Its checks have been progressively later, or smaller, with an outstanding balance looming larger—dangerously large, if it is a primary customer. You, as the business owner or accounts manager, have pushed the nagging worry to the back of your mind and continued to provide products or services with regular billings.

The Small Business Administration rates the inability to collect monies owed as the second most common cause of new business failure, outranked only by undercapitalization.

The National Association of Credit Management (NACM) has some eye-opening figures for the business owner who thinks the company can stay on top of collections without carefully planned systems that include contingencies for slow and no payers. The NACM says that as the length of time between initial billing and receipt of payment stretches on, the value of your accounts receivable dollar shrinks to 67¢ in just the first six months of delayed payment, then to an anemic 47¢ at the end of a year, and on down to a "why bother?" 4¢ in five years. By the end of six months, one third of the billed dollar is gone, making the point painfully clear that prompt payment is serious business.

If you are already in business and have no established collection policy, or if your business is in the "about to be" stage, the time to set up an effective program is now, before you open those doors. If you have an established business, take this time to review your current collection policy.

Develop a Collection Policy Early

In spite of the obvious, many new business operators spend a great deal of time gaining expertise in their specialty and no time learning to collect compensation efficiently for that specialty. Accounting procedures must be as carefully prepared as the selling of the product itself if the business is to succeed.

The main ingredients in a quality collection policy are clarity and consistency. New customers receive a clear contract, in simple but precise terminology, explaining the type of service they are buying, how much they will pay for that service, and the terms of payment. The contract is in writing whenever possible.

Trouble-free collection starts at the front office, where sales and service personnel aim for clarity in all of their dealings with customers. A customer who buys because he has been dazzled by the verbal maneuvers of a facile sales rep may present so many problems when the reality of billing hits that the company would have been better off not to have gotten the sale at all. It's fine to use colorful methods to grab attention, but sales pitches must stop before the new customer signs a contract committing your company to its needs. This is when contracts are produced, plain English spoken, and the nitty gritty of expectations, prices, and terms determined.

Once clarity is established and the new prospect has become a paying customer, a file is begun on its account, and the next step, consistency, becomes the important factor. Every client is a favored customer. Bills, payout periods, and dates for follow-up billings and phone calls should be a consistent company policy. Later, when time proves that some customers are consistently good payers (meaning payment within 30 days), they will reap the benefits of discounts for prompt payment. If your company is solid and cash flow is strong, these customers might enjoy the extension of short-term credit.

Conversely, an extremely poor payer may have to be put on C.O.D. terms or make deposits before its orders are filled. Again, though, these are not exceptions to your rules, but rules set up to treat exceptional cases. A collec-

Case: Getting Paid

The Placers, a Wilmington, Del., temporary personnel and permanent job-search firm, found that 60% to 70% of its delinquent accounts were actually owed by its regular customers. Many of them were past due 60 to 90 days or longer. The company had been growing so fast that its payroll supervisor had only 15 minutes a day to spend on collections.

Founder and president Alan Burkhard looked at five areas ripe for accounts receivable reorganization:

1. Manpower and training. He hired and trained two people to handle billing and collections. He scripted their approaches carefully and made sure that collection staffers had a customer-service orientation.

2. Customer communications. Within 15 minutes of every new sale, a customer-service rep calls the customer to go over the order, explaining payment terms.

3. Reference checks. New clients' references are now checked quickly by phone, not by mail.

4. Invoicing and follow-up. Customer-service calls are now made less than 10 days after invoices are mailed to flag any problems that might indicate payment slowdowns. Reps also ask clients to commit to a payment date.

5. Companywide cooperation. The accounting department now coordinates its activities with sales, customer service, and other key departments.

As a result of putting new policies and procedures in place, The Placers was able to push delinquent bills down to about 5% of sales, compared with about 15% previously.

tion procedure that is fair and consistent across customer lines is as necessary as quality products. These policies will save the day when overdue accounts begin to need special attention or aggressive collection.

In the interests of a uniform collection policy, specialized procedures can be set up right at the beginning that reward prompt payment and penalize dawdlers. Many new companies are unfamiliar with such techniques, even though they are common practice lately among established businesses and very easy to institute. The sample invoice below shows a customer how much money is discounted from its bill by prompt payment. "2/10 net 30" means

Invoice

ABC Manufacturing
1 Narrow Road
Anytown, USA

Invoice Date_____

Invoice Number_____

SOLD TO:	**SHIP TO:**
XYZ Distributors	XYZ Distributors
10 Broad Street	10 Broad Street
Anytown, USA	Anytown, USA

Terms: 2/10/N 30	Customer Order No.		Shipped VIA		
QUANTITY			Unit		
Ordered	Shipped	DESCRIPTION	Price	Amount	TOTAL
1	1	Widget	$23.30	$23.30	
3	3	Doohickies	98.95	296.85	
		Subtotal			$320.15
		Tax @ 4%			12.81
		Total Due:			332.96
		Discount (2/10)			6.66
		Thank you.			

A 2% monthly service fee will be charged on all unpaid balances after 30 days.

that a customer can take a 2% discount if payment is received within 10 days, but the entire balance must be paid in 30 days. This is based on the simple idea that you, the billing company, stand to earn money by the interest you can generate on a positive cash flow. Margins gradually fade when funds are outstanding for as little as 10 days beyond the due date of the bill.

The concept behind discounts is that savings realized by early payment are passed on to the customer at a current rate. Using the same reasoning, the billing company loses money for holding an account payable for more than 30 days in most cases. Thus, a small interest charge begins to accrue against the customer's account after the 30th day. The fact that the value of accounts receivable, as we mentioned previously, begins to erode rapidly after only 30 days makes this the sensible policy. *Caution:* As mentioned in the previous chapter, some customers take the discounts and pay late; others may ignore the late payment charges and still pay late.

Work on Potential Problems Right Away

In spite of our best efforts on behalf of impeccable billing policies, problems still develop. In the introduction, it was mentioned that the Small Business Administration identifies the inability to collect monies owed as the second most prevalent cause of new business failure (the first was undercapitalization). To those of us trying to collect our bills in a timely manner, this means that too many new businesses, including a few that may become our customers, start with too little money. Because of a survival policy of waiting to get paid for deliveries to their own customers before they pay their suppliers, they often make poor payers themselves, routinely taking 60 to 90 days or longer. The only way to come out on top with such a company is to avoid its business when possible.

The previous chapter, "Credit and Collections," focused primarily on methods for determining the creditworthiness of new customers. A thorough discussion of credit is beyond the scope of this chapter, but a few key items are worth mentioning. Briefly, if you are in the position of taking on a company with no established reputation, be sure to check the company's status with its existing business colleagues, its bank's estimation of ability to pay, and most certainly, the authority of the contact person. If a new customer is going to become a delinquent account, chances are it has already done so with another vendor.

Let's assume we have now set up collection policies, established the reputability of potential customers, and still, routine checking of invoice dates turns up an account that is 30 days from the date of original billing with no payment received. Here is where good record keeping will save your billing department. Remember when the file was begun on the new account? If possible, such files should be computerized for easy storage and retrieval to make routine checks easy. Ideally, you would check the status of these files daily. If time is short or staff at a premium, visit these files no less than once a week. On the 30th day, action commences immediately.

Due to the extent of payment problems today, and because in collection, time is money, action taken on accounts 30 days past due often starts with a phone call after an initial reminder. Ask to speak to the company officer directly responsible for accounts payable. Identify yourself and ask for that person's name. Names establish accountability. Get a firm commitment as to date, amount, and method of payment. Be polite, but steadfast, and don't allow the passage of more than 10 days before the payment of some part of the balance. Above all, always treat the party from whom you are asking payment with respect. There are specific channels of redress available if it does not act as promised. No collection problem excuses bad manners or the issuance of threats.

One successful collection agent suggests the use of sales techniques. She recommends the kind of careful listening, sincerity, and understanding of the customer's situation as expected from the sales representative when he or she first tried to sell the product. A top collection lawyer reflects a similar attitude in his transactions. Whenever possible, he tries to end a collection procedure on a positive note. Clarity and honesty of presentation in collection of bad debts are not only good business, they are the law. Tough consumer protection measures in most states now protect the indebted's right to be free from harassment. Follow up the phone conversation with a letter itemizing the agreement made, and put a copy, along with a notation of the phone call, in the customer's billing file. To avoid accusations of harassment, don't call or write again until the agreed upon time limit is past, then do so immediately. This kind of impeccable collecting practice will usually inspire the respect necessary to win both payment in full and continued good company relations. If it doesn't do it, stronger steps will need to be taken, but this does not change your attitude of compassion and fair dealing throughout.

The Client Who Can't Pay

You will eventually encounter the client who, for a variety of reasons not immediately resolvable, simply can't pay the bill. Assuming you have followed the recommended procedures up to now, the incidence of "can't pays" will be few, and the matter can be attended to in a way that does damage to no one's business image or self-esteem beyond temporary inconvenience. From your previous attempts to collect, the basic information needed has been established, and you are ready for positive action. Everyone knows whether the customer is dissatisfied, playing for time against temporary cash flow problems, or, the worst, going broke. Assuming you were clear and consistent in all prior dealings (and rapport is still good), the facts are that this customer needs immediate attention. By now, no more products should be going out to this account except on a C.O.D. basis. Sometimes arrangements can be made for a portion of past-due money to be added to each C.O.D. until the account is current.

In most cases, the customer will have already ceased ordering, which brings us to a variety of other workable techniques for compromise. The most obvious is an adjustment in terms. Given an extended payment period of smaller monthly installments (or weekly if prudent), the entire past-due amount will likely be collectible over time. Arrange adequate interest to be included in the payments. Remember, carrying this account out more than just six months will result in the loss of a third of your money if no interest is charged. A reasonable customer (and most are) will recognize your need to protect yourself from undue losses.

Installment plans and interest bring up another excellent solution: transfer of debt. Most small businesses can't afford long-term debt collection, even on behalf of a prime client, but professional lenders can. Try to transfer the debt, perhaps to a MasterCard or Visa account. The idea should motivate the debtor, who will recognize two options: meet the obligation to your company or incur the higher penalty in interest that a professional lender will charge. The choice could mean fewer inconveniences or hard feelings for both of you.

By the time everything else has been tried and the debt begins to look lost, consider canceling full balance in favor of partial payment. Losing some is better than losing all. Partial payment compromises are underrated as acceptable last-chance alternatives to litigation. Lawsuits are so costly in both money and bad company relations that the returns, usually only a portion of the debt by the time the lawyer is paid, are a Pyrrhic victory at best. However distasteful, though, legal action can become necessary in a minority of cases and must be considered as a collection final resort for the rare company that will not cooperate on another solution.

The Client Who Won't Pay

Both professional collection agents and attorneys agree that inability to pay the bills, whether it happens to a company or an individual, is unintentional and unmalicious. Therefore, the client who *won't* pay is usually a dissatisfied customer. Clear contracts and impeccable practices will help you ward off this kind of trouble. But suppose it happens. An unhappy client, especially one who still owes money, is a public relations problem because it feels compelled, often by guilt, to explain to your mutual business contacts why it has not paid. Compromise the difficulty, perhaps by rendering additional unbilled service or by canceling all or part of the balance, if possible. If these solutions don't fit the magnitude of the situation, outside arbitrators can be asked by both parties to render a judgment that is binding. The Better Business Bureau runs a professional arbitration service in many towns that is free to its area businesses.

At this point in the process, every conceivable avenue has been exhausted for an amicable solution, and still you feel justified in your collection attempts. Seek professional intervention, either through a collection agency or an attorney, if you're sure you are in the right and the amount justifies the hassle. A reputable and effective agent or attorney may be able to arrange payment without going to court by the use of the same techniques described above, combined with his or her professional clout. Another possible alternative is small claims court, where judgments are easy to win but hard to collect.

After having won a court judgment, you have the right to attach a debtor's assets with a lien. The problem with such drastic measures is, again, the ill will incurred and the time it can take to collect. A debtor does not have to pay a debt secured by a lien until it wishes to dispose of the encumbered assets. It could take years.

What's the Best Way to Avoid Problems?

Prevention is the best cure for what can become a serious malady. Anyone can call a lawyer and go to court. The good business habits that underlie every collection technique stressed here are those same qualities we hope for in all aspects of business and personal life. The qualities of business impeccability are clarity in all customer dealings (both verbal and written), consistency in all company practices with every customer, honesty, patience when the payment can be so critical that even 10 days hurts, and compassion—put yourself in their shoes, and remember that unexpected events can cause any company to have temporary financial difficulty. No one intends to become a bad debt. The more sensitivity that can be brought to bear in collection while still maintaining effectiveness, the better and more profitable the resolution.

Automated Accounts Receivable

Ideally, you want to know which of your customers pay on time and who the slow payers are. Then you can devote your attention to servicing your best customers. A basic accounts receivable system (whether automated or not), gives you this information, especially if you age the accounts. This means listing the receivables by due dates. Normal aging is Current, 30 days, 60 days, and more than 60 days.

Of the vast number of small businesses with less than $5 million in sales, only about 5% have computerized accounting systems. Many businesses simply have no need for a fully automated system, particularly if the number of customers and the amounts of receivables are small. For those businesses, a tickler file will suffice.

A basic tickler file works this way: When an invoice is sent, you enter the amount of the invoice, along with accurate customer information such as address, billing contact, etc., under the appropriate date due (30 days in most cases). At the beginning of each day, you can call up the invoices due on that particular day and proceed from there.

Identifying what your business is and where it might be headed could be number one on the list for determining whether you need an automated system. Do you see yourself expanding in the future so that the time spent in entering figures to your ledger will become overwhelming? Also, what else would you want the system to do for your business? Are there accounting packages you need other than accounts receivable? Any system needs to be matched with what you would like it to accomplish.

Many businesses that could benefit from the use of a more sophisticated accounts receivable system are scared off by the idea of automating their accounts, either because of cost or the stories they've heard about setting up such systems. However, there is plenty of software currently on the market emphasizing both simplicity and lower cost. QuickBooks and M.Y.O.B. are only two examples of a wide collection of software packages specially designed for small businesses.

If you are toying with the idea of automating your accounts receivable (or other accounting applications such as general ledger, accounts payable, payroll, etc.) the first logical person to check with is your accountant. Your accountant probably uses an automated system and can fill you in on the type of financial package in use for your particular business. He or she can help you select a program that is compatible with the methods currently in use, help you locate a dealer that sells that particular software, and may actually be interested in helping you set up the system. You are, after all, a good customer, and automating your books may make his or her work more efficient. Few computer dealers have accounting expertise.

Armed with professional advice, one final suggestion is to buy locally if possible. Accounting software is well-known for demanding a bit more hand-holding at the initial start-up stage than other software packages. Having an expert available at a moment's notice can make the whole process run smoothly. Proper support is the key to whether the system works—and works well.

Remember that the important idea behind purchasing the system is to make your accounting procedures easier and more accurate, so you can devote your time where it counts: tending to your most profitable customers.

Action Plan

Collection of Accounts

❏ Develop a collection policy based on clarity, consistency, and courtesy.

❏ Set up an aging system to track all accounts, whether delinquent or not.

❏ Computerize your system; set up due dates for follow-up action. A tickler file is better than no system at all.

❏ Work on potential problems right away. Delays cost you money.

CHAPTER 15

Inventory Management

For most businesses, inventory is the largest current asset on the balance sheet. It ties up cash and affects taxes. Managing inventory can be a time-consuming task or a relatively trouble-free one. It all depends on the systems you have in place.

Inventory management software has taken much of the drudgery out of the task. Consequently, such techniques as economical ordering quantities, optimal stocking levels, and break-even analysis will be used by more and more businesses of all sizes.

The basic ideas are straightforward: You want to buy inventory as inexpensively and economically as possible. Too little inventory results in stockouts or interruptions on the work floor. Too much inventory results in heavier storage, handling, insurance, and financing costs, to say nothing of the increased risk of ending up with stale, outdated, or damaged goods.

How much inventory do you really need? How much can you afford? What timing should be considered? What method of monitoring inventory is appropriate for you?

These are tough questions for any business to address. But they must be answered. They can spell the difference between a profit and a loss once you add up the total cost of inventory management errors.

Review Purchasing Decisions and Procedures

Inventory management begins with careful purchasing. You can avoid most of the problems associated with inventory management if you establish clear routines to follow when ordering any new or additional inventory.

Look at how purchasing decisions are made in your business. Who makes the purchasing decisions? On what basis? The decisions must make good business sense. Any item to be put in inventory for resale, for instance, should be an item that you expect to sell in a reasonable period. Inventory turn is all-important, particularly when the carrying costs of inventory are so high.

The same management principles that govern the rest of your business apply to the purchasing process. One person has to be responsible for purchasing. Dividing this responsibility without a good business justification creates problems. In a large business, many people may be involved with purchasing—but the same concept holds. You must be able to identify the person who makes the decisions, and that person must have the authority to match the responsibility.

Cost/price decisions must be made: Find out who makes them. Selecting merchandise for resale should be done within a budget: Find out who sets a budget—and when. Who makes the decisions?

Once these questions are settled, another set crops up—one more directly tied to the actual management of purchasing. You need answers to the following questions:

1. Do you use purchase orders?

Even the smallest company should use standard purchase orders (POs), numbered sequentially. They help you control purchases, determine how well suppliers meet delivery schedules, and provide positive evidence of what you ordered and when. POs help you time future purchases, and they provide raw data for further analysis.

Annual inventory carrying costs can run as high as 30% when you consider:

■ Insurance

■ Financing

■ Working capital

■ "Opportunity costs"

■ Taxes

■ Storage

■ Security

■ Handling

2. Do you use blanket purchase agreements?

Investigate blanket purchase agreements for anything that you buy in large quantities. If, for example, your company buys huge amounts of sheet metal during the course of a year, your supplier might be willing to guarantee a bulk price if you contract to purchase a minimum amount during the year. You can have it delivered when you wish. If you can arrange this kind of purchase, it benefits all parties concerned. It improves your cash flow (lower costs, bills due only upon delivery of goods, predictable level of Cost of Goods Sold, no unanticipated price increases during the contract period, and so forth). Suppliers benefit because they know that your company will buy so many tons of that particular sheet metal, and they can plan accordingly.

3. Have you established economic ordering quantities?

Economic ordering quantities (EOQs) are established by studying the costs of ordering and maintaining an inventory. The major assumption here is that inventory use is uniform. If you have erratic inventories, this method may be inappropriate. Ask your accountant to help you set EOQs. Different principles apply to different businesses, and your costs have to be determined—you may not have the figures readily available. However, if your inventories are used in a uniform manner over the year, and if they are substantial, EOQs can result in major cost savings.

Your accounting software may include an EOQ program. Since so many businesses use EOQs profitably, many electronic spreadsheets and inventory management programs incorporate EOQs as a routine offering.

4. Are stock lists available from your major suppliers?

Many distributors distill their experience in their industry into stock lists for customers. These lists can help you decide what to order, help keep you aware of what other businesses like yours are purchasing, and provide other important insights.

5. Have you set minimum and maximum stock points for specific items?

You can avoid overstocking if you set a maximum stock level on certain items. It also becomes easier to resist "bargains" on slow-moving items. It is more difficult to avoid understocking, but minimum acceptable stock levels help prevent stock-outs and work-flow interruptions.

Review minimum and maximum points frequently—and rejustify them periodically to prevent buying out of sheer force of habit.

6. Do you take advantage of discounts?

You should. On an annualized basis, 2%/10 days works out to 72%—a substantial amount. Ask your banker to help you work out the details. You may find that you actually save money by borrowing to take advantage of discounts.

7. Are purchases made on a dollar-available basis?

This can be a danger sign. If your working capital is so tight that you are on a C.O.D. or cash-only basis with your suppliers, then you may have some major problems. In some cases, recapitalizing the business is the only answer, but there may be other options such as securing new debt, reducing costs, or increasing productivity.

If you are put on a cash-only or C.O.D. basis by your vendors, check into it immediately. Was a payment inadvertently missed?

8. Are purchases made only in reaction to pressing needs?

This is another possible danger sign. Purchasing departments should anticipate needs, not react to them. While this is not always possible, there should be an earlier warning than customer complaints or stock-outs to initiate the purchase of new inventory.

9. Do you review reorder levels at least annually?

Set reorder points to prevent stock-outs—and then review them. This is one of the best ways to avoid overstocking obsolete or slow-moving items. But don't set reorder levels and then blithely forget them. Check them, and then check the rationale behind them, one by one.

Inventory management starts with careful purchasing decisions. What—and how much—do you need to have in inventory? Who makes these decisions? On what grounds? Are well-tried tools such as EOQs, reorder points, and blanket purchase agreements being used? If not, why not? Are discounts being sought? Are the basic danger signals observed?

Establish Reorder Times

Establish reorder times by looking back at sales cycles and vendor delivery times, and looking forward to anticipated sales and/or manufacturing forecasts.

1. Timing Based on Experience

What looks to an outsider like speculation may, for an experienced buyer, be a very carefully planned order. If you have years of experience in a particular field, then the patterns or cycles of that field become second nature.

Thoughts like "These stocks look low; next month is when the demand will boom; the supplier takes three weeks; better order tomorrow..." flash through your mind.

If you don't have the experience, or if you want to make sure that others in your business understand the process, you'd go through the same steps. First, what are the stocks now? What kind of turnover do you anticipate? Do you have enough stock on hand to meet that demand? What are the reorder times? When should you place the order?

2. Reorder Points

Set reorder points on standard items—whether for resale or assembly, for parts or office supplies. Reorder points simplify matters by doing the analysis once. It can then be applied again and again. Some consultants specialize in helping you set reorder points. Other help is available from suppliers, wholesalers and distributors, trade associations, and (in some areas) competitors.

Reorder points are great time-savers, but they do have limitations. They depend on somewhat flexible cash flow. Sales levels fluctuate, and distribution patterns and suppliers may change. If your cash flow is flexible enough, you can accommodate reordering at any time and nothing interrupts the smooth flow of commerce. But you should consider these questions: What level of stock-outs can you afford? How often and in what inventories?

3. Standing Orders

Standing orders with principal suppliers may be another solution. If you use blanket purchase agreements, standing orders may be appropriate. Otherwise, they suffer from the same defects as standing reorder points. They

---

Material Resource Planning

The Material Resource Planning (MRP) method allows you to work backward from the time you need to have all the necessary materials delivered. Write down the length of time it takes to get each needed item (see below). If, for example, you need power cords from Taiwan and cases from China, you can list the times involved and mark them on a chart as shown on page 158.

Lead Times for Ordering Materials for Space Heaters

Item	Lead Time (Weeks)
Case	8
Fan	5
Harness	4
Switch	4
Power cord (120V)	3
Base	2
Heat coils	2
Dial	1
Handle	1
Screws	1

The case obviously takes the longest time to receive, so it becomes the governing item from which all others are "backed off" in terms of ordering time. The figure on page 158 shows the ordering schedule for the various parts. The case is ordered on the very first day; three weeks later, the fan is ordered, a week later than that, the harness and switch are ordered, and so on.

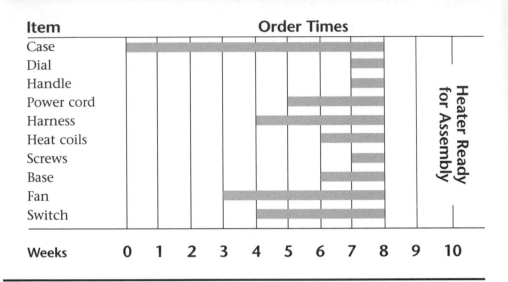

Item	Order Times										Heater Ready for Assembly
Case											
Dial											
Handle											
Power cord											
Harness											
Heat coils											
Screws											
Base											
Fan											
Switch											
Weeks	0	1	2	3	4	5	6	7	8	9	10

also share some of the same benefits: They are simple, inexpensive, and, for stable businesses, effective. But once again, tough questions come up: What inventories can you take a chance with? What level of stock-outs can you afford—and in which inventories? (There are statistical techniques to help make these decisions more comfortable.) Once you are able to detect a cycle, including looking at the best and worst cases, you will ordinarily be able to set standing orders for the most stable items.

Most businesses use a combination of these three methods—because they have a mix of inventories, some of which can be managed speculatively, some on experience-based hunches, some on standard reorder points, and some on standing orders. The right mix will be a balance. If that balance has been carefully established, your chances of success are greater than if you rely on any one technique.

Check Inventories Consistently

Once you have established purchasing and timing policies for the inventories your business needs, managing the physical inventory becomes an ongoing process. Some of the common systems for controlling inventories are listed below. All are means to the same end: keeping the right inventories on hand, in the right amounts, at the right times, at the right costs.

Most businesses use a combination of these systems, since the amounts involved (and the inventory values) vary widely. Use your judgment on which ones are right for your business, and if you are not certain, call in a professional to help you make the decision.

Physical Count

Take physical counts periodically—monthly or quarterly—to make sure that balances tally with what your books say should be there. If there are serious deviations, you may have a security problem, pilferage, excessive breakage or wasting, or other problems that can easily slip by unnoticed without periodic physical counts. Any other control methods are variations on this theme and must be compared at some point to an actual count.

But you don't need to take physical counts of everything at the same time. Critical inventories or those of unusually high value should be more carefully attended to than others. This is a matter of managerial judgment.

Your inventory turnover ratio helps you achieve a balance between overstocking and understocking.

The formula is:

$$\frac{\text{Average Sales}}{\text{Average Inventory}} = \text{Inventory Turnover}$$

Compare this ratio with industry standards and act on deviations. Too low a ratio may mean your inventory is too large; too high a ratio may indicate that you are not carrying enough in stock.

Your banker or accountant can provide you with industry norms. One source is the Robert Morris Associates Annual Statement Studies. Another is your industry association and trade group publications. Sometimes you can trade information with businesses similar to yours, but that are in different markets.

"Eyeball" Control

The simplest and most common method: The stock looks low, reorder. If it doesn't, let it ride. While this is a low-cost method, it provides no systematic controls and no obvious method of improvement (except to switch to a more formal system). Since it depends on snap evaluations, it can lead to unnecessary stock-outs. For some inventories (office supplies, for example) it may be sufficient. For production or resale inventories, it's usually too simplistic.

"Brown Bag" and Bin Reserve System

If you know the acceptable minimum levels for parts and other inventories, this system works fairly well—particularly when there are large numbers of small parts that are kept in bins or on shelves.

In a brown bag or in a separate closed part of the bin or shelf, stow away the acceptable minimum. When the bin or shelf is emptied and the brown bag must be opened (or the reserve tapped), reorder. There are many variants to this simple system, including the use of checklists and a reorder storage area (where the reserves are kept).

"If you can free up cash from inventory," says Howard Skolnik of $10-million Skolnik Industries, "you can spend it on growth instead."

Thanks to a closely controlled inventory operation, Skolnik can ship most products to customers within 24 to 48 hours of ordering. And inventory levels are leaner than they were when his Chicago-based company was half its current size.

The company's financial-reporting system tracks these five trends:

1. *Gross margin return on investment.* Manufacturing units subtract the costs of a product's raw materials, direct labor, and factory overhead (including warehousing costs) from their selling prices, and divide that by the selling prices. (Administrative costs are left out.) The goal on each manufacturing product line was set at a 15% to 25% rate of return. For distributors, which lack production expenses, the ratio is calculated by subtracting the costs of goods bought from goods sold, and dividing that by selling prices. A distributor's goal should be a 25% rate of return.

2. *Inventory turnover.* As a rule of thumb, manufacturers' inventories by product line should turn over six to eight times a year. Distributors' inventories should turn over four times a year. Slower than that, and too much cash is being tied up in a warehouse. Skolnik aims for a turnover rate of about eight times annually. He also tracks finished and "online" goods on a weekly basis, reserving monthly reports for raw materials only.

3. *Percentage of orders shipped on time.* Lean companies may not always be able to fill orders as promptly as they would like, but Skolnik aims for a 98% success rate at fulfilling orders within the promised terms.

4. *Length of time to fill back orders.* Skolnik dreads backlogged orders so much that he pays extra to do business with suppliers that can make emergency deliveries when he receives unexpectedly large orders. His accountant advises him to increase inventory and production in some cases to avoid increasing the time it takes to fill back orders.

5. *Percentage of customer complaints to shipped orders.* A complaint ratio higher than 2% could signal problems. At that point, it's essential to analyze each complaint for what it could reveal about operations. Incorrectly shipped items may indicate a poor product-tracking system, mislabeled storage bins, or badly trained warehouse personnel. Consistently late shipments may also signal computer overload.

Perpetual Inventories

If you know what inventories you begin with (by actual physical count, checking against deliveries and making sure you get what you ordered), and if you know what you are using up or selling, then this kind of system makes the most sense—because as inventories are consumed, the perpetual inventory changes.

These systems can be simple: Use cash register or sales slip information, and lower inventories accordingly. When new shipments arrive, check the goods against the POs and shipping documentation, and increase inventory records accordingly. Periodically, run a physical count to make sure that the perpetual inventory figures are accurate.

These systems can be complex. Many stores use a tag system or a bar code system to monitor inventories electronically: As a sensor is passed over the code, changes in the inventory are automatically recorded. In manufacturing plants, where there are at least three kinds of inventories (raw material, work in progress, finished goods), the systems are even more complicated and call for professional help to set up.

Computerized Inventory Management Systems

Parts Inventory Management Module

- Materials requirements and planning report
- Parts invoice valuation
- Over/understock
- Adjust register

Production Scheduling and Control Module

- Production work
- WIP-PWO sequence (Work in Progress-Production Work Order)
- Production scheduling report
- Monthly production report

Finished Goods Inventory Control Module

- Inventory valuation and gross margin report
- Adjust register
- Over/understock
- Order desk report
- Cost of sales

The great strength of perpetual inventories is the information they can provide. If you can tell, at any time, exactly what you have on hand (or should have, according to a working perpetual inventory system), purchasing and timing decisions are greatly facilitated. Slow-moving items can be isolated, and unnecessary stock levels can be reduced to free up working capital and make better use of floor or shelf space.

Case: Tracking Return on Investment (ROI)

Avoid getting stuck with product that doesn't move: Find out how to analyze the profitability of inventory. Gerard Badler, principal of Gambit Group, analyzed the inventory in his brother's New York store, Maurice Badler Fine Jewelry. First, they looked at each item's inventory ROI, comparing item profitability with how much was being carried, and then looked at the ROI per item broken down by how long it had been held (note: dollar amounts and dates are for example only).

Step 1: Calculate ROI of inventory

	Gold earrings	Silver bracelets
Annual Gross Profit	$50,000	$40,000
Average Cost of Inventory on Hand	150,000	50,000
Return on Investment	33% (50,000/150,000)	80% (40,000/50,000)

Most profitable: Silver bracelets

Step 2: Calculate age-specific ROI to identify which older items need to be moved

Item: Gold earrings. Average cost of inventory on hand: $150,000
Gross profit over one year: $50,000, or 33% (50,000/150,000)

To cover administrative and selling expenses, the store needs a gross profit return on inventory investment of 75%. Since the store is getting only a 33% return, the investment doesn't look like it's paying off. At first glance, it looks like the gold earrings aren't profitable enough to keep on hand. But, when breaking down the profitability by how long it's been in stock (age of receipt), we see that the older stock is dragging down the profitability. Here's how to calculate the age-specific ROI:

1. **On-hand inventory cost:** Find out how much is paid for all the items on hand that were purchased during a specific period of time.

2. **Profit:** Calculate the profit from selling this product during the last 12 months.

Age	Inventory Cost	Gross Profit ($)
First half of 1999	$20,000	$40,000
Second half of 1998	70,000	10,000
First half of 1998	10,000	0

The age-specific ROI is the ratio of gross profit achieved during the last 12 months to on-hand inventory cost for merchandise received during a specific time frame, multiplied by 100.

Time Period/Age-specific ROI
First half of 1999/200%*, second half of 1998/14%, first half of 1998/0%

*Since this inventory group was not available for more than six months, the ROI should be annualized. Assuming no seasonality, this number is 400%!

These examples show a dramatic drop in profitability over time. The new stock is profitable, the older stock needs to be moved. Conclusion: Avoid the drop in profitability by more aggressively discounting the item as it ages. Age-specific ROI needs to be constantly monitored as customers' tastes change, as customer-demand limits are reached, and as the effects of promotion and discounts sink in.

Action: Put more money into silver bracelets, and reduce inventory of gold earrings.

Computerizing Your Inventory

Computers lend themselves to inventory management. The most obvious application is in perpetual inventory systems, but there are unlimited additional possibilities.

Some of the systems are integrated with full accounting systems; others are straightforward inventory management systems that are designed around your inventory information needs. As an indication of what you can look for, see the box on page 161. These simple menus are just a hint at the kind of help you can get from a computerized inventory system.

However, you will still have to take occasional physical counts. There is no substitute for them. All that other systems do is provide time-saving alternatives for actual physical counts.

Summary

If you lower the Cost of Goods Sold, keep carrying costs to a minimum, and prevent stock-outs and interruptions due to parts or material shortage, then your inventory system will work well. But as your company grows and processes change, you will have to review all management systems, including inventory.

Some danger signs to heed are stock-outs, customer complaints, damaged or lost goods, sudden quality control problems, lowered production, and higher Cost of Goods Sold. There are others—but those listed here are particularly clear signals that need immediate attention.

Careful inventory management doesn't have to be expensive or complex, but it does need to be thorough and consistent. Periodic reviews will keep your inventories under control and increase your company's profits.

Action Plan

Inventory Management

❑ Review purchasing decisions and procedures. Answer the questions on pages 154, 155, and 156.

❑ Establish reorder times.

❑ Check inventories consistently.

❑ Review procedures and costs. A computerized inventory management system is likely to pay for itself.

Resources for Small Businesses

Check out your local library, bookstores, and these sources of small-business management information. Some of the titles listed here can be readily obtained using several different search engines on the Internet, such as www.abebooks.com or www.bibliofind.com.

Books

Accounting

Activity Accounting: An Activity-Based Costing Approach, by James A. Brimson; John Wiley & Sons, 1997. This book outlines an activity accounting approach to cost management. (Softcover, 224 pages, $39.95.)

Bottom Line Basics: Understand and Control Business Finances, by Robert J. Low; Oasis Press, 1994. Guides you past the mechanics of accounting to an understanding of financial management to improve cash flow, reduce costs, and give you a clear idea of what is driving your business. (Softcover, 306 pages, $19.95.)

Business Owner's Guide to Accounting & Bookkeeping, by Jose Placencia, Bruce Welge, and Don Oliver; Oasis Press, 1997. Makes understanding the economics of your business simple. Explains the basic accounting principles that relate to any business. Step-by-step instructions for generating accounting statements and interpreting them, spotting errors, and recognizing warning signs. Discusses how creditors view financial statements. (Softcover, 172 pages, $19.95.)

Financial Statements: A Step-by-Step Guide to Understanding and Creating Financial Reports, by Thomas Ittelson; Career Press, 1998. Shows step-by-step how non-accountants can understand and create balance sheets, income statements, and cash flow statements, and how to use them to make good decisions. (Softcover, 200 pages, $15.99.)

How to Understand Financial Statements: A Nontechnical Guide for Financial Analysts, Managers, and Executives, by Kenneth R. Ferris, Kirk L. Tennant, and Scott I. Jerris; Prentice Hall, 1992. For entry- to intermediate-level financial professionals, this book provides plenty of theory and practice of use to small-business people as well. (Hardcover, 306 pages, $39.95.)

The Portable M.B.A. in Finance and Accounting, 2nd Edition, by John Leslie Livingstone; John Wiley & Sons, 1997. Informative coverage of financial statements, forecasting, budgeting, pricing, tax issues, acquisitions, exchange rate risk, and much more. (Hardcover, 524 pages, $32.50.)

Banking and Finance

The Bankers: The Next Generation, by Martin Mayer; Truman Talley Books/Dutton, 1997. A survey of the current and future state of banking. (Hardcover, 514 pages, $29.95.)

Borrowing to Build Your Business, by George M. Dawson; Upstart Publishing, 1997. A book for borrowers and about lenders. Includes detailed guidelines on selecting a bank and a banker, answering the lender's seven most important questions, how your banker looks at a loan, and how to get a loan renewed. (Hardcover, 144 pages, $16.95.)

Financing Your Small Business: Techniques for Planning, Acquiring, & Managing Debt, by Art DeThomas; Oasis Press, 1992. Essential techniques to successfully identify, approach, attract, and manage sources of financing. Shows how to gain the full benefits of debt financing while maintaining its risks. Outlines all types of financing and carefully walks you through the process—from evaluating short-term debt options to negotiating a long-term loan, to deciding whether to go public. (Softcover, 274 pages, $19.95.)

Finding Your Wings: How to Locate Private Investors to Fund Your Venture, by Gerald A. Benjamin and Joel Margulis; John Wiley & Sons, 1996. Includes a useful analysis of what investors look for in angel deals and a valuable section on the due-diligence process. (Hardcover, 266 pages, $34.95.)

The Small Business Insider's Guide to Bankers, by Suzanne Caplan and Thomas M. Nunnally; Oasis Press, 1997. With an inside look at how bankers operate, this book does an excellent job of explaining how to search for the right bank and fine-tune the perfect loan proposal. (Softcover, 176 pages, $18.95.)

Budgeting

Budgeting Basics and Beyond, by Jae K. Shim and Joel G. Siegel; Prentice Hall, 1995. This is a combination overview and step-by-step guide to budgeting, including insights on software packages such as Lotus and Excel. Includes real examples in manufacturing and service business situations. (Softcover, 464 pages, $24.95.)

Business Planning

The Guide to Retail Business Planning, by Warren G. Purdy; *Inc.* Business Resources, 1996. Developed exclusively for the owners and managers of retail businesses. Detailed step-by-step instructions and do-it-yourself worksheets provide the expert guidance you'll need to create and organize your winning plan. Samples of actual business plans of successful retail companies and a comprehensive resource directory help you identify and find the key information you need. (Softcover, 250 pages, $19.95.)

How to Really Create a Successful Business Plan, by David E. Gumpert; *Inc.* Business Resources, 1997. Guides you step-by-step with detailed chapter-end exercises along with analyses and critiques of real-life business plans. You'll learn how to target objectives, secure financing, garner contracts, attract key staff, and merge or acquire companies. (Softcover, 212 pages, $19.95.)

The Service Business Planning Guide, by Warren G. Purdy; *Inc.* Business Resources, 1996. Developed exclusively for the owners and managers of service businesses. Reviews business planning essentials, arms you with trade/media contacts, and provides tips for using the Internet to build your plan. Includes three complete business plans, one venture plan, worksheets, a resource directory, and forms for each step of the service business planning process. (Softcover, 336 pages, $19.95.)

The Start-Up Guide: A One-Year Plan for Entrepreneurs, 3rd Edition, by David H. Bangs Jr. and Upstart Publishing, 1998. A practical framework to research and test ideas inexpensively, define and identify ways to reach the best markets, forecast sales and expenses, and use the Internet as a source for low-cost resources. (Softcover, 192 pages, $22.95.)

Management

Competing in the Third Wave: The Ten Key Management Issues of the Information Age, by Jeremy Hope and Tony Hope; Harvard Business School Press, 1997. Insights on management guidelines for strategy, customer value, knowledge management, business organization, and market focus, from real business stories. (Hardcover, 252 pages, $27.95.)

On Your Own: A Woman's Guide to Building a Business, 2nd Edition, by Laurie Zuckerman; Upstart Publishing, 1993. *On Your Own* is for women who want hands-on, practical information about starting and running a business. It deals honestly with issues like finding time for your business when you're also the primary care provider, societal biases against women and credit discrimination. (Softcover, 332 pages, $18.95.)

Running and Growing Your Business, by Andrew J. Sherman; Kiplinger/Times Business, 1997. A good manual for understanding the strategic, financial, and legal aspects of today's competitive marketplace. (Hardcover, 368 pages, $25.)

Start, Run, and Grow a Successful Small Business, edited by Susan M. Jacksack, J.D.; CCH, 1997. A valuable reference and compendium of tips and strategies on all aspects of small business. (Softcover, 704 pages, $24.95.)

Periodicals

Harvard Business Review. This venerable publication contains helpful articles on entrepreneurship and other management issues. $85 per year. 800-274-3214.

Inc. magazine. The leading small-business magazine for growing companies (38 Commercial Wharf, Boston, MA 02110); $18 per year (18 issues). 617-248-8000. For subscription service, call 800-234-0999 or 303-604-1465.

Small Business Forum: Journal of the Association of Small Business Development Centers. Case studies and analyses of small-business problems gleaned from a national network of small-business development professionals. Includes book reviews. Reprints available. University of Wisconsin, SBDC (432 North Lake St., Madison, WI 53706; $25 per year (3 issues).

Internet/Web-based Resources

Here's a small sampling of Web sites that illustrate the breadth of small-business resources on the World Wide Web. Browser software, such as Netscape Navigator or Microsoft Internet Explorer, is needed to access these sites.

Bureau of Economic Analysis: www.bea.doc.gov
This agency of the U.S. Department of Commerce offers estimates of regional, national, and international economic data.

Business Resource Center: www.morebusiness.com/products/shareware
A list of links to shareware and demo software in the following categories: finance, legal, project management, spreadsheets, inventory management, business planning, and marketing.

CAP Automation: www.capauto.com
The Web site for a software developer that specializes in retail management, including POS (Point of Sale) software.

Claris Small Business Central: www.claris.com/smallbiz
A Web site providing expert advice, helpful articles, and resources on start-up, funding, tax management, and marketing.

CPAFirms.com: www.cpafirms.com
Magal & Albrecht Partnership, in Bowling Green, Ohio, maintains this site, which lists CPA firms by region, along with their Web sites.

Datamatics Management Services: www.datamaticsinc.com
This company offers software for payroll processing.

Dun & Bradstreet Resource Center: www.dbisna.com/resources/menu.html
News, resources, and links with relevance to small and start-up businesses.

Economic Statistics Briefing Room: www.whitehouse.gov/fsbr/esbr.html
This page of links provides easy access to current federal economic indicators.

Gateway Publishing's Internet Sourcebook.Com: www.internetsourcebook.com
This site includes detailed company profiles, career resources, and discussion forums, all focusing on technology companies.

Inc. Online, the Web Site for Growing Companies: www.inc.com
This extensive site contains material from the archives of *Inc.* magazine, plus bulletin boards, resources, and links of interest to small and growing businesses.

Internal Revenue Service (IRS): www.irs.ustreas.gov
This site is a handy route to Uncle Sam's tax forms and tax-related publications.

Northwestern Mutual Life Small Business:
www.northwesternmutual.com/business/advisors/accountant.html
A good resource of links for small-business accountants.

Quicken Small Business: www.quicken.com/small_business
Everything from small-business news to resources for small-business management.

The Conference Board Leading Economic Indicators and Related Composite Indexes:
www.tcb-indicators.org
Links to historical and current composite indexes of leading, coincident, and lagging indicators.

U.S. Census Bureau's Census Economic Briefing Room:
www.census.gov/briefrm/esbr/www/brief.html
This site summarizes and links to an extensive series of government economic indices, including chart versions.

University of California GPO Gate: www.gpo.ucop.edu/info/econind.html
This Web site provides access to U.S. economic indicators as prepared monthly for the Joint Economic Committee by the Council of Economic Advisors.

R. Walters & Associates Accounting Software Directory:
www.accountingdirectory.com
A listing of accounting software publishers, titles, and resource directories for those looking for accounting systems.

Organizations

Center for Entrepreneurial Management (29 Greene Street, New York, NY 10013). A nonprofit association for small-business owners, CEM maintains an extensive list of books, videotapes, cassettes, and other small-business management aids. Call 212-633-0060 for information.

Colleges and universities. Most have business courses. Some have Small Business Development Centers, others have specialized programs. Some have small-business expertise and 170 now offer specific courses in entrepreneurship.

Comprehensive Accounting Corp. (2111 Comprehensive Dr., Aurora, IL 60507) has more than 425 franchised offices providing accounting, bookkeeping, and management consulting services to small businesses. For information, call 800-323-9009.

Keye Productivity Center. Keye Productivity, a division of American Management Association (11221 Row Ave., Leawood, KS 66211), offers business seminars on specific personnel topics for a reasonable fee. Call 800-821-3919 for topics and prices.

National Association of Credit Management (8815 Centre Park Dr., Columbia, MD 21045) is a network of 75 associations offering educational seminars and credit-reporting, collection, and adjustment bankruptcy services. (310-740-5560)

SBT Corp. provides software services and support for accounts receivable. (800-227-7193)

Service Corps of Retired Executives (SCORE), sponsored by the Small Business Administration, provides free counseling and a series of workshops and seminars for small businesses. Of special interest: SCORE offers a Business Planning Workshop, which includes a 30-minute video produced specifically for SCORE. As of June 1999, there were 389 SCORE chapters nationwide. For more information, contact the SBA district office nearest you, or log on to SCORE's Web site at: www.score.org.

Small Business Administration (SBA). The SBA offers management assistance programs and Management Assistance Officers. Any local or district SBA office is worth a visit, if only to leaf through its extensive literature. For openers, call 800-U-ASK-SBA—the "Small Business Answer Desk."

Small Business Development Centers (SBDCs). Call your state university or the Small Business Administration to find the SBDC nearest you. By far the best free management program available, the 900+ SBDCs provide expert assistance and training in every aspect of business management.

Glossary

Accounts payable: A liability resulting from a purchase of goods or services on an open account.

Accounting cycle: The process accountants use to produce an entity's financial statements.

Accounts receivable: Amounts owed by customers as a result of delivering goods or services and extending credit in the ordinary course of business.

Accrual basis: An accounting basis that recognizes the impact of transactions on the financial statements in the time periods when revenues and expenses occur.

Aging of accounts receivable: Analysis of individual accounts receivable according to how long since they have been billed.

Assets: Resources that have monetary value, such that they should benefit future cash inflows or help reduce future cash outflows. Assets can include intangibles such as goodwill.

Audit: An in-depth examination of transactions and financial statements made in accordance with generally accepted auditing standards.

Bad debt: Receivables either determined to be unrecoverable, or that would cost more to collect than the debt is worth.

Balance sheet: A financial statement that shows a company's assets and liabilities at a particular instant in time.

Budget: A forecasting of revenue and expenditure for period of a business's activities.

Capital: Capital funds are those that are needed for the base of the business. Usually they are put into the business in a fairly permanent form such as in fixed assets, plant, and equipment, or are used in other ways that are not recoverable in the short run unless you sell the entire business. Capital also identifies the owner's equity in a proprietorship or partnership.

Carrying cost: The cost of holding stocks, machines, and factories. The carrying cost is the amount that cost of assets could earn if it were sitting in a bank instead.

Cash flow: Usually refers to net cash provided by operating activities; there is also cash flow from financing, investing, and operating activities.

Cash flow statement: A required statement that reports the cash receipts and cash payments of an entity during a particular period.

Certified public accountant: An earned designation achieved by a combination of education, qualifying experience, and the passing of a two-day written national examination.

Collateral: Something a borrower provides as security for a loan.

Compound interest: Interest rate multiplied by a principal amount that changes within a given period. The unpaid interest is added to the principal to become the principal for the new period.

Cost accounting: Breakdown of the costs of manufacturing a product or of producing a service.

Cost of capital: Calculation of the relative costs of different types of capital, such as loans, equity, and bonds.

Cost of goods sold: The original acquisition cost of the inventory that was sold to customers during the reporting period.

Credit: An entry or balance on the right side of an account.

Credit rating: Assessment of the creditworthiness of a company, individual, or a debt instrument. Moody's and Standard & Poor's provide credit ratings for many large entities.

Current assets: Cash plus assets that are expected to be converted to cash or sold or consumed during the next 12 months or within the normal operating cycle if longer than a year.

Current liabilities: Liabilities that fall due within the coming year or within the normal operating cycle if longer than a year.

Current ratio: Current assets divided by current liabilities.

Debit: An entry or balance on the left side of an account.

Debt: Debt refers to borrowed funds, whether from your own coffers, other individuals, banks, or other institutions. It is generally secured with a note, which in turn may be secured by a lien against property or other assets. Ordinarily, the note states repayment and interest provisions, which vary greatly in both amount and duration, depending upon the purpose, source, and terms of the loan. Some debt is convertible, that is, it may be changed into direct ownership of a portion of a business under certain stated conditions.

Debt-to-equity ratio: Total liabilities divided by total shareholders' equity.

Debt-to-total-assets ratio: Total liabilities divided by total assets.

Depreciation: The systematic allocation of the acquisition cost of long-lived or fixed assets to the expense accounts of particular periods that benefit from the use of the assets. This allows accountants to spread the cost of plant and equipment over a number of years, instead of charging them all against the profit of the year in which they were bought.

Direct cost: A cost that is directly attributable to the production of a product, and varies in direct proportion to the number of units produced.

Direct method: In a statement of cash flows, the method that calculates net cash provided by operating activities as collections minus operating disbursements.

Discounted cash flow: A way of calculating the present value of a future stream of income and capital; used to compare different expected rates of return on different projects.

Discounts and allowances: The reduction in the price of merchandise or services to customers based on classification of the customer (i.e., commercial vs. individual) and/or volume of sales activity. Allowances are typically offered to retailers by manufacturers (e.g., retail display allowances).

Double entry: The fundamental principle of bookkeeping and accounting that dictates that every entry in a company's books have an equal and opposing counterpart. Every business transaction has an credit on one side of the ledger and a debit on the other, and the two must balance. To put it another way, at least two accounts are always affected by each transaction.

Economic order quantity (EOQ): The order quantity, based on the fixed costs of placing an order and the associated inventory-carrying costs, that minimizes the total cost of an item.

Equity: The financial interest of all shareholders in a company. Unlike capital, equity is what remains after the liabilities of the company are subtracted from the assets—thus it may be greater than or less than the capital invested in the business.

Financial Accounting Standards Board (FASB): A private-sector body that determines generally accepted accounting standards in the U.S.

Financial accounting: The field of accounting that serves external decision makers, such as stockholders, suppliers, banks, and government agencies.

Financial statement analysis: Using financial statements to assess a company's position and prospects.

First in, first out: Commonly known as FIFO, it assumes that the oldest production inputs are used up first, for accounting purposes.

Fiscal year: The 12-month period for which a company draws up its financial statements. Many companies have excellent reasons not to use a calendar year as their fiscal year.

Fixed asset: Assets that remain in a business over time, like office buildings, factories, and land. Fixed assets do not include inventory, raw materials, or expendables used to make other goods.

Fixed cost: A cost that does not vary with the amount of goods or services produced. Rent and bank interest are two examples.

Forecasting: A company's guesses about what will happen in the future. Examples are general predictions about the economy, or about the company's markets, or about the direction of costs or sales.

General ledger: The record that contains the group of accounts that supports the amounts shown in the major financial statements.

Generally accepted accounting principles: A term that applies to the broad concepts or guidelines and detailed practices in accounting, including all the conventions, rules, and procedures that together make up accepted accounting practice at a given time.

Goodwill: The intangible but valuable asset (i.e., reputation) of a business that is developed from the sale and/or distribution of useful merchandise or services. Also, community involvement by the business to promote the public good.

Gross profit: The difference between sales revenue and cost of goods sold.

Gross sales: Total sales revenue before deducting sales returns and allowances.

Income statement: A report of all revenues and expenses pertaining to a specific time period.

Indirect cost: A cost that cannot be directly attributed to a particular product. These costs have to somehow be allocated to a particular product in order to calculate the price at which the product can be sold profitably.

Indirect method: In a statement of cash flows, the method that adjusts net income to reflect only cash receipts and outlays.

Intangible assets: Rights or economic benefits, such as goodwill, patents, brand names, trademarks, and franchises, that are not physical in nature.

Interest: The rental charge for the use of principal.

Interest rate: The percentage applied to a principal amount to calculate the interest charged.

Interim periods: The time spans established for accounting purposes that are less than a year.

Internal control: Refers to both internal administrative control and internal accounting control.

Inventory: Goods held by the company for the purpose of resale.

Inventory shrinkage: Difference between a) the value of the inventory if there were no theft, breakage, or losses of inventory and b) the value of inventory when it is physically counted.

Inventory turns: A ratio of sales to inventory. A "turn" equals sales divided by inventory value. The greater the number of turns, the more efficiently the business's inventory dollars are being used.

Internal rate of return: The interest rate at which the discounted future cash flow from a project exactly equals the investment in the project. For the project to be worth investing in, the internal rate of return must be higher than the marginal cost of capital.

Journal entry: An analysis of the effects of a transaction on the accounts, usually accompanied by an explanation.

Last-in, first-out: An inventory method that assures that the units acquired most recently are used or sold first, commonly known as LIFO.

Leading and lagging indicators: Indicators that come before the economic event they are forecasting are leading indicators; indicators that confirm economic activities after they have occurred are lagging indicators.

Ledger: A group of related accounts kept current in a systematic manner.

Leverage: Borrowing money for a business venture to produce an expected return higher than the cost of the borrowed funds.

Liabilities: On a balance sheet, the opposite of assets, representing economic obligations of the organization to outsiders, or claims against its assets. Assets minus liabilities equals net worth, which is the company's underlying value to shareholders.

Line of credit: Either secured or unsecured, an agreement that ordinarily is renewed on an annual basis where a bank holds funds available for the use of a business. Usually an unsecured line will have to be completely paid out once a year.

Limited liability: A feature of the corporate form of organization whereby corporate creditors ordinarily have claims against the corporate assets only. The owners' personal assets are not subject to the creditors' grasp.

Long-term liabilities: Obligations that fall due beyond one year from the balance sheet date.

Liquid assets: Any assets that can be turned into cash without loss, such as bank deposits or government securities.

Loan agreement: A document that states what a business can or cannot do as long as it owes money to (usually) a bank. A loan agreement may place restrictions on the owner's salary, dividends, amount of other debt, working capital limits, sales, or number of added personnel.

Margin: The difference between the total cost of an item (including overhead costs) and its retail or selling price.

Modified Accelerated Cost Recovery System (MACRS): The basis for computing depreciation for tax purposes in the U.S. It is based on arbitrary "recovery" periods instead of useful lives.

Net income: What remains after all expenses have been deducted from revenues.

Net worth: A company's assets minus its liabilities.

Notes payable: Promissory notes that are evidence of a debt, and state the terms of payment.

Operating expenses: The amounts paid to maintain and/or operate a business, such as the cost of utilities, supplies, taxes, depreciation, and insurance.

Operating income: Gross profit less all operating expenses.

Operating management: The management of major day-to-day activities that generate revenue and expenses.

Owners' equity: The residual interest in, or remaining claim against, the organization's assets after deducting liabilities.

Paid-in capital: The total capital investment in a corporation by its owners at the inception of business and afterward.

Partnership: A special form of organization that joins two or more individuals together as co-owners.

Payback period: The time it takes for an asset or investment to pay for itself.

Percentage of accounts receivable method: An approach to estimating bad-debt expense and uncollectible accounts at year-end using the historical relations of uncollectibles to accounts receivable.

Percentage of sales method: An approach to estimating bad-debt expense and uncollectible accounts based on the historical relationships between credit sales and uncollectibles.

Perpetual inventory system: A system that keeps a running, continuous record that tracks inventories and the cost of goods sold on a day-to-day basis.

Pro forma statement: A carefully formulated expression of predicted results.

Product costs: Costs that are linked with revenues and are charged as expenses when the related revenue is recognized.

Profit center: A self-contained part of an organization that is responsible for generating its own profits and/or losses.

Quick ratio: Calculated by dividing current liabilities by current assets, this is an informal indication of a business's ability to meet its financial obligations. It is also known as the "acid test" ratio.

Replacement cost: The cost of replacing an asset today. Accountants frequently value a company's assets at their replacement cost.

Return on capital: Relationship between the net profit of a business and the paid-up share capital of the business.

Return on total assets: Income before interest expense divided by average total assets.

Revolving line of credit: Similar to a line of credit, except it needn't be paid out annually. This kind of loan is of particular interest to a rapidly growing company with weak capitalization, and it may be converted to a term loan under certain conditions.

Risk analysis: Banks often analyze a company's financial risk according to factors such as the variability of cash flow, the growth of cash flow, the relationship to interest payments, the company's debt maturity over the next year, and its liquidity.

Short-term investment: A temporary investment in marketable securities of otherwise idle cash.

Short-term liquidity: An organization's ability to meet current payments as they become due.

SKU (stock keeping unit): Inventory items of the same style, color, and size.

Straight-line depreciation: A method that spreads the depreciable value evenly over the useful life of an asset.

Subordinated debt: The holders of this form of debt have claims against only the assets that remain after the claims of general creditors are satisfied. For a bank's purposes, subordinated debt is as good as capital, so they sometimes refer to it as "quasi-capital."

T-Accounts: Simplified version of ledger accounts that take the form of the capital letter "T."

Tangible assets: Physical items that can be seen and touched, such as land, natural resources, buildings, and equipment.

Term loans: Either secured or unsecured, usually for periods of more than a year, to as many as 20 years. Term loans are paid off like a mortgage: so many dollars per month for so many years. The most common uses of term loans are for equipment and other fixed asset purposes, working capital, and real estate.

Trade accounts payable: Obligations resulting from purchasing goods and services on credit.

Trade discounts: Reductions to the gross selling price for a particular class of customers to arrive at the actual selling price.

Trial balance: A list of all accounts with their balances.

Working capital: This is the difference between current assets and current liabilities. Contrasted with capital, a permanent use of funds, working capital is for relatively short-term use. Since it consists of a variety of forms—inventories, accounts receivable, cash and securities—working capital may fluctuate.

Write-down: A reduction in carrying value to below cost in response to a decline in value.

INDEX